Shadow and Gateway Theory

This publication is designed to provide accurate and authoritative information regarding the subject matter covered. While the publisher and author have used their best efforts in preparing this book, they make no representations or warranties with respect to the accuracy or completeness of the contents of this book and specifically disclaim any implied warranties of merchantability or fitness for a particular purpose. The advice and strategies contained herein may not be suitable for your situation. You should consult with a professional when appropriate. Neither the publisher nor the author shall be liable for any loss of profit or any other commercial damages, including but not limited to special, incidental, consequential, personal, or other damages.

No portion of this book may be reproduced in any form without written permission from the publisher or author, except as permitted by U.S. copyright law.

New York, NY
United States of America
© 2026 Baruch Menache
Published by McWest & Associates
All rights reserved.
ISBN: 978-1-971928-02-9

Shadow and Gateway Theory

Transitional Between Extremes

Baruch Menache

AUTHOR'S NOTATION: 1

INTRODUCTION 7

PART ONE: THE STRUCTURAL SHADOW 9

THE DUALITY OF THE SHADOW LOCALE 11

THE ROLE OF THE SHADOW LOCALE IN CIVILIZATION 15

SCALABILITY AND STRUCTURAL LATENCY 19

GOVERNANCE OF THE SHADOW 21

THE INTERLACED SHADOW: REPRESENTATION AND ASCENT 25

THE INTEGRATED SHADOW 33

PART TWO: THE CONCEPTUAL SHADOW 43

CONCEPTUAL SHADOW AND SOCIABILITY 45

CONCEPTUAL VS. GENUINE SHADOWS 49

TRAGIC FORM AND DISCONTINUITY 53

PART THREE: THE SUBJECTIVE EXPERIENCE OF THE SHADOW 55

ENTERING THE SHADOW LOCALE 57

DREAD, DUALITY, AND SOCIAL BECOMING 67

LIMITS OF PERCEPTION 73

SHADOW OF ASCENDANCY 75

SHADOW PERSONA 83

SHAME, MEMORY, AND FRAGMENTATION 93

PART FOUR: SHADOW AND THE CORPORAL FUNCTION 101

SOCIAL PERSPECTIVE AND SEQUESTERED FORM 103

SHADOW AND INSTITUTIONAL PROTECTIONISM 109

THE DISRUPTIVE SHADOW 119

PART FIVE: BEYOND THE SHADOW 121

DISENFRANCHISING THE SHADOW 123

THE PROTECTIVE AND DEGENERATE SHADOW 131

TOWARD INTEGRATION 137

PART SIX: GATEWAY LOCALES 143

GATEWAY AS CONTAINER AND IMAGINATION 145

GATEWAY AS INFRASTRUCTURE 149

DOORWAY AND DISRUPTED CONTINUITY 153

MASCULINITY AND THE DOORWAY 159

DOMAINS, FOUNDATIONS, AND CONCEPTUAL DISAGREEMENT 163

DEPENDENCY AND PASSAGE 165

CONSCIOUS FLOW AND BIOLOGICAL EXPERIENCE 171

GATEWAY OF SOCIALITY: PERFORMANCE AND POLITICS 177

PERSPECTIVE, DIVERSITY, AND IMAGINATION 185

Author's Notation:

This work is merely the study and theory of an approach that a psyche or an infrastructural setting can take. Effectively, that is the choice of the beholder, and either to be traditionally developed, placed on by circumstance or any other sort of process. Although being an approach does not exempt the notion that it is without choice that the approach was taken, it is the case that it can be removed just as a hat can be removed from one's head. It is not based on individuals or based on the criteria of their intrinsic nature, since it is rather an approach towards specific aspects. Many of the theories developed are based on the author's own experience in this approach, rather than utilizing a subject matter for which they are more inclined to take this approach. It is not in any way a reflection of the individuals that take up an approach or of infrastructure which follows the succession of these theories.

More so, this is theoretical in nature, philosophical in origin, and thus not the practical manifestation of social details. It does not coordinate with reality as it manifests, but merely consists of suppositions that have an altogether different practical manifestation. The purpose is for greater understanding, not greater practical development for the individual or group, since such development would require their own volition to develop their intellectual apparatus according to how they see fit, and especially in how they manifest in the realm of activity.

Although it would seem that a specific subject would be more inclined toward such an approach, this is simply based on tradition, circumstantial process, and other orientations. It is not the individual themselves; it is not their genealogy, their biology, their intellectual apparatus, or any sufficient condition thereof. Orientation of individuality is merely an approach to life, an approach to consciousness, an approach to systems.

This approach that will be articulated is found to be an existent of nature preceding that of humankind and is only manifested in humankind based on the choice of such beings to take that approach. We will study the human being because that is a reference point, but it is not the source of that reference, but rather an important subject matter that allows for more understanding of the theory, not more understanding of the individual whom takes precedence of that approach.

The individual themselves supersede such an approach and have the ability, and are naturally inclined, to change approaches across different life stages. If we find a subclass to be more oriented toward this approach, it is not for the understanding of that subclass, but for the understanding of this theoretical framework.

It is also for all that are oriented, whether under this approach or outside of it, to understand its relational ability and its coordination, not for active change, but rather through its understanding, and thus in what way one sees fit to approach individuals and process. It is for individuals to protect themselves from orienting toward systems that are less understood, as well, for individuals who are in such systems to orient themselves within and external to those systems; it is in no way exemplifying such subjects.

The individual themselves, their genealogy, is the basis for the ability of any approach, and we have not developed theoretical frameworks as in what way specific biological systems are better adapted to different approaches. It is not that we cannot derive such suppositions, but it is altogether not about the understanding of biological differences, but differences in approaching reality for the amicability of any individual as they see fit.

We are for the advantageous development of individualistic, group, and societal process, not for understanding for its own sake; although the understanding is for its own sake and is not stately to individual activity, which requires a thorough analysis of personal regard and not within the scope of our subject. The individuals that happen to be under the subclass that may be inclined toward such an approach are very arbitrary to the nature of this work; rather, it is in how they perform this approach that is our only inquiry; in what way they deviate from or assent to it. It is as if we are studying a fashionable item and its extension of the individual, but in no way is it the study of the individual themselves. It is mere clothing of regard, despite the consequences and advantages of the approach.

It will relate back to the individual because the approach inevitably intersects with one's individuality, but the simple removal or change of an approach would change its intersection with the individual. We are not ascribing human value or differences of value, but rather proclaiming the understanding of an approach and its associated value in the chain of social process, in the same way we would understand a labor-intensive item to contain a higher market value. So too, different aspects of that approach would have different value. If we are ever to ascribe value, it is only because of the aspect of that approach. It is because of the labor itself, and not because of the individual that lies behind the labor.

If one is seeking to understand for practical manifestation, or to understand a subclass for itself and not for the theory, then I guide them away from this work, because they are seeking to understand social process for reasons other than the development of a theoretical framework, especially in relation to how it manifests in their own personal process. The individual, whoever they are, does at one point or another take an approach of the shadow, as does the child, as well as any other approach, such that there is no reason to assume that a subclass in relation to the shadow is the true origin. They have merely taken that approach; it is not them, but in how they have acclimated toward it, and more so that it is a significant study; thus proving the purposeful need of its exemplification, much like another other approach or theoretical framework.

It is a consistent and formalized theory; it has its disadvantages and advantages and is thus of no substantial moral nature. It merely has a namesake that would assume it to be a disruptive force, but it is only such if applied in a social setting in a particular manner. In this theoretical framework, we are simply understanding sequential process for its sake, without offering positive or negative attributes, but only consequences and advantages. As usual, it is with more understanding that we develop as individuals, as a society, or as a group, not with less understanding.

As such, if the argumentation is lacking or if it requires more in-depth research, then it is for the reader and the researcher to take up that journey and disregard the ideas set forth if they do not succeed in argumentation and development as a theoretical framework. If they do not succeed as a purposeful agenda for ultimate practical manifestation, then I disagree. Of course, any tool can be utilized improperly, but in this case it is required that one understand more of these theoretical frameworks to understand how they intersect, especially in a realm where social process has become more complicated, thus requiring more understanding.

Theories have always been used to the detriment of society as well as for its benefit, and it is according to the individual that they take up this process. I have described these terms and theoretical processes in a manner separate from social dictation, and I would ask the reader to do the same in their perception. We are following an institutional parameter of this discussion, as though in a psychiatric hospital in the woods; to develop and understand for the benefit of the theory itself, and to be forgotten in relation to other social beings and their process.

Baruch Menache

Introduction

In other works, we have noted the two extreme locales: the central locale and the interactive one. We have elaborated on how the interactive locale can be embodied or simply interactive, and the necessary ramifications of each. In the present inquiry, we are to note two other locales, similar to fall and spring, in that they are not fully defined but are distinct enough to recognize and process their elements. We must make it clear at this moment that all locales are present in every locale and we are only concerned with a generalized version of events as they would appear, as well, to determine the most dominant, for which there will only be one.

For example, the interactive locale has a center, and the central locale has interactive properties. We are only demonstrating the structural organization to which we are all bound, showing that there is a definite system where there is a central locale, such that its interactive pockets are to be considered central. Conversely, there is an interactive locale that will be considered such even within its center. To this, we now turn to the other two which serve as transitions between these two extremes.

One will serve the transition away from the central locale, and the other will serve as the ascendency from the interactive locale. The former will be termed the "shadow" locale, in that it is not an interactive pocket since it does not adequately separate from the central locale. It is also not a central locale because it is somewhat separated from that domain. The latter will be termed the "gateway," in that it serves to remind and perform as the area of structure that leads from the interactive locale to the central locale.

These locales do not retain the provisions of the central locale, as they are structurally separate. Nor do they serve as distinct interactive locales, as they lead to an ascent or descent pertaining to the central locale. These two pseudo-localities are required in the performance to serve against the regular process of either the central locale or the interactive locale. Because they lack the ability for concrete stability, and more so, when one takes residency in this locale, we require a proper system in place.

PART ONE: THE STRUCTURAL SHADOW

The Duality of the Shadow Locale

There are two differentiating approaches to the shadow: one is a default manifestation of a shadow in a manner of participation with conscious experience, or as an emblem of a shadow in its perspective upon the overwhelming experience of consciousness. For example, any form of animated domesticity or high interactivity that is coerced into the perceptual arena would automatically become the shadow; for it represents itself as the details that make up the consciousness experience and thus not only redundant but disruptors to the flow that carries an assumption of an already perfected domestication.

This would be the default shadow to any conscious experience, such that in any locale, if a couple is over-interactive, especially concerned with domesticated elements against the backdrop of other patrons, it would be a default manifestation of a shadow to that locale. We do not need to study the establishment where it is situated. Simply by the fact that there is a coerced interactivity from these two patrons, it has an expectation, more so, a conscious layer of some sort, that such patrons will represent the under-structure of that system; being as who they are as existent beings, and, more so, who are the others.

A sophisticated shadow locale is the creation of a shadow format in its reflection of a wholesome conscious experience.

It is a situation that only reflects the true nature of consciousness. It does not do so because it coerces interactivity all the while being structurally connected to consciousness, but rather because it finds itself actualized in contrast to the consciousness experience. Surely, the way to actualize in contrast to consciousness is by a high level of domesticity or interactivity while maintaining a position in a consciousness space; but that is merely to assist and reflect, creating an aura of a whole-sum reflection of that state.

The difference would be that one who is situated in such a locale would automatically experience their individuation formatted upon the representational setting. While in the default shadow experience, it merely disrupts the regular circumstance and expectation. As with the patrons and the establishment, the other patrons will find a disruptive experience rather than a representation of their domesticated elements; having been presented for the perceptual experience. It is simply that they seek to have an established experience, with such as being disrupted of that. Once they depart, they no longer have that participation or its shadow elements.

However, in a shadow locale, one that is engineered to participate in the whole-sum reflection and contrast of consciousness, it will be the case that one who enters such a domain not only experiences their domesticated elements formatted as a representation, but also becoming intertwined with the actualization that goes against their entire structure. This would have them begin to degenerate into their various parts, especially in the matter in which they have connected to consciousness; with the final outcome having them scattered in their makeup. This is not a real degeneration but rather an experienced degeneration, as one does not lose the conscious attachment but rather is compelled to pay heed to the contrast, and through that contrast one can endeavor to ameliorate the substance; such to reach out in a better manner toward genuine consciousness.

A more illustrative example would be a haunted house or the notion of infrastructure that has a representational effect but does not heed to its purported sociality or connection to existential infrastructure, which would be a formatted shadow locale, in which one will automatically experience their inner demons, or in other words, a psyche breakdown of the conscious substance in its differentiated format. No one can keep away from that experience at the entrance of that domain.

Differing from that would be a locale that provides service but rather interest in an interactive format with an individual instead of its expected representation; a direct communication from individual to individual. In this case, it would be an exemplified experience of the shadow, so that one would be disrupted from the conscious experience of the moment. But it is not to represent the breakdown or degeneration of one's psyche, but rather the fact that there is a disruption in the conscious flow.

Similar to how a barrier, gateway, or doorway, all the activities of separating domains, could all be considered shadows in some sense because they do in fact purport an interaction that is void of the representational format. It is interacting to tell you not to interact. That is why a doorway is closed: for it interacts by dictating, "Do not enter," or "Do not go through this place," for then it would not be a gateway but rather an open space. A single shadow can be considered the separation or disruption between two conscious possibilities, experiences, or expectations, and alternatively considered as a fully formatted domain of the shadow, and each experience utilizes the elements of the other.

The question becomes: can one create the experience of a domain that is formatted as a shadow simply by noticing the shadow elements? One can find themselves in the experience of a haunted sense in many locales, whether such might be in agreement by the social realm or not. What would that mean to have one create the shadow locale, and are there any limitations to that possibility?

First, we should notice the elements of the locale that purport to be representational but do not fit the infrastructure dynamic that is supposedly connected to it. For example, a large house that is fairly empty or unoccupied, purporting to be a representational element to provide a haven for a high degree of sociality, but with actual sociality not being existent to provide that inference of infrastructure. Could it be the case that one could enter into a very small locale or structure and find elements that purport a representational element but do not connect to an infrastructure? If one pays heed to that, they would be able to find a shadow element and thus a shadow locale in any environment.

The Role of the Shadow Locale in Civilization

No one can depart from a civilized structure once they have obtained that very attachment. Any attempt to separate from the civilized structure will only be a representation of the critique against the civilized structure in the embodiment of a new actualization. When one thinks they are producing a formalized civilized entity, they are rather producing the very elements that are critical of the prior civilization.

This is how we can produce an individual, locale, or group that can obtain to be the environment of the shadow in corresponding to the civilized structure, whether or not they are participating in a shadow locale. It is only a matter of considering what civilized structure they have already obtained to understand how they embody the actualization that is thus critical of that very system.

When one produces such a state in which they cover themselves as a new entity but yet are only producing the shadow of the civilized structure, they become the embodiment of that shadow. This would mean that, in taking the role of the shadow, the only things that truly permeate their psyche are interactivities against that representation. Like any shadow locale or individual embodiment of a shadow, it provides a perspective of a representation without it being an actual representation, such that one experiences their actual state. The shadow, in essence, provides the realization that true individuality only comes when one becomes self-conscious, or, in other words, without consciousness itself but rather a certain reflection of consciousness, which is enabled in the shadow locale.

This is why we find that the embodiment of a shadow turns its visuals into erratic interactive systems; they find bitterness in the state of their constant individuality and the dysfunctions that permeate at the depths of their domestication. This has no alternative because they neither bear a representational quality of their own or distinct separation from that initial representation. They do not endure domesticity; they have a form that appears like domestication, but it is rather the in-between of domestication and consciousness. Hence, we term it the shadow because it exists between domesticated separation and consciousness continuity.

There is really no salvation within the shadow locale other than the performance of individuality for the necessity of gaining a better understanding or amelioration, but this sort of individuality becomes corrupted in itself because one cannot handle or deal with the depth of domestication, which generates resentment and bitterness.

We can gain a better understanding from the environment of the shadow or a shadow locale to comprehend the civilized component in terms of both its vulnerability and its substructure. Therefore, the shadow locale does serve a purpose to society and to sociality, as being an informant, albeit usually on the negative component, like a shadow does, but an informant of consciousness sentiment.

One can find that, without any form of shadow or the embodiment of shadow, or the avoidance of shadow locales, one will lose perspective of the substructure of the civilized element and make erratic formulations or fail to realize its core components. Therefore, the shadow does serve an essential function in giving credit and validation to the understanding of the civilized element, so that one realizes its vantage point that is neither within the civilized element nor from the domestication.

This is different from the gateway locale, which does not provide a perspective of the civilized element since it partakes in the civilized structure itself and therefore does not become aware of its vulnerabilities, nor does it understand its obstruction because it is the thing itself.

In fact, if we take a more comprehensive view of the subject, we would notice that without darkness or the shadow of sunlight, we would not understand sunlight as we do, but rather as a simple system that is virtually in effect. It is possible that we would perceive the sun no differently than a star in the sky because of its lack of availability for that awareness. Something else might take the effect of the shadow to provide a nuanced perspective of the sun, whether its governing abilities or its substructure, but rest assured that it would be downgraded as a core element without the existence of the shadow.

Scalability and Structural Latency

When there is a change of scale between the upper tier and lower tier of a system, the attributes in the larger scale are removed from the equation, and in turn the epicenter of the scale incorporates those attributes. What is left of the broader scale is structurally inhabited with the ability of obtaining those attributes. Because of the changing scalability, it must convert into a shadow system. It cannot refer back to a new version of a lower-tier scale because its effect on the infrastructural status remains as though it were participating at a higher degree of scalability. Although the individual may be able to access a more articulated version of their new position albeit with assistance, they are not able to maintain their infrastructural and perceptual experience, as well as social exchange. This is the result unless there is an immediate infrastructural separation or a social amendment that is agreed upon by all constituents; to portray that change of scalability.

The change in scalability alongside an infrastructural and social proclamation, is but a long-standing and complicated foundation as a lifeline between the two. Because of this, any complex system will naturally incorporate a bearing of this latency, which would be the case that the shadow is prevalent from the outset and cannot be mediated unless humanity is at its perfection.

Governance of the Shadow

I stand corrected, in that it appears that without the shadow there is no ability to access information at any level of complexification. It may be seen that it is almost of the attention, whether public or private, to ascertain the shadow element, for if not relegated, one will be without true socialization or experience separate from corporal systems. In fact, very much the grievance of governance is an overextension into avoiding the shadow elements, such that governance creates for itself a corporal structure throughout its society. Thus, not only is it corporal in its own extension as a political structure, but as well it has created the entire mainframe of the state to participate in a corporate system, without the ability of entering into socialization; the arena that is outside the corporal system. This has the state becoming completely dependent on whatever little socialization does take effect within its borders, and especially external to its borders; including the socialization of higher altitude that does transform and transpire the entire corporal system upon which it is dependent.

In fact, any domineering system or agency will have the ability, and very much so to act upon it, to dispel the shadow element. This is because it is perceived as the downtrodden state of the amicability of that internal system. They do this because they assume a thorough realization of the particulars that exemplify themselves as the shadow, as though needing particular attention toward that sphere, and in that way attempt to dispel that very shadow.

If they are successful, as they usually are, the shadow element they create for the entire system establishes a corporeal structure that withdraws from socialization and is therefore not considered a dynamic system, unlike a system that would require a superego or guiding agency. The corporate structure does not lead, for it is outside of sociality, but simply constructs itself based on its corporal articulation; and leadership is simply the detail of that articulation, more so than in any way being domineering or hierarchical.

Hierarchical systems within a corporal structure are systemized as an ironic function, since it is as though there is no hierarchy, so that there is a proclamation that there is in fact a hierarchy in place; as though we need to create one which would naturally not be presupposed.

The higher the hierarchical system of a familial body, for example, the shallower of an exemplified as such, for it is naturally predisposed to such suppositions, and therefore is a redundant sentiment to proclaim it. Whenever we do find an approximating hierarchical system, we can assume that such is strictly corporal, for it needs to articulate its function because it is not naturally presupposed to that hierarchical exchange within sociality; where there is no sociality existent within its mainframe.

There may be an attempt to exemplify the shadow foremost from the onset, as though in allowance for the accession of that detriment to play out, so much so that what is beyond the shadow has the opportunity of existing, whether or not it does stand forward in its ability to be beyond the shadow. The risk of such an approach is that, many a time, the entire populace or constituent becomes very much entrenched within the shadow elements, for it is both persuasive and difficult to distinguish what is beyond such parameters, more so to actualize outside such a realm when it is rampant with participation in shadow elements. Even without acknowledgment or awareness, one will attempt to escape outside of the shadow elements which have been proclaimed from the onset. But because of the details that constantly make themselves known, as well as the localities to which such shadow elements systemize themselves, it is almost a requirement of a mental game in addition to a very controlled geographical settings, for one to be successful in remaining in a real arena that is thus able to be an extension outside of the shadow elements.

To find that locality, whether geographical or psychological, is already a task in itself, such that it is almost the entire pedigree of the beginning stages of social extension to find oneself at least not deeply influenced or actualized by the shadow elements, and then to proceed to the particulars of that social development. In that process, one can easily, in the avoidance of the shadow elements, take position within a corporal structure, for it is easily assumed to be the safe haven of protection from shadow aspects, since it neither agrees with the shadow nor includes it within its parameters. But it is the case that the corporal structure does not include a shadow, much like it does not include any sociality, because it is not functional as an organization within social parameters. Thus, it is a realm of protection, for it is of no realm in any existential consequence.

The Interlaced Shadow: Representation and Ascent

The shadow constitutes a combination of representational aspects alongside interactive elements, comprising a shadow by the one entering by way of the representational aspect. This is to behold the contrived interactive elements that do not intersect properly, or to the elusiveness of that representation. If one entered via the interactive state, they would either be content with the supplementary representational themes, or, more so, become an animating provision for the regular state of interactive privatization.

Then there is a third entrance, through the beholden nature of performing in themselves as a formal shadow, that they are most aligned when interacting with another shadow reserve. They embody the disparity between representations and interactivity in a combination they wish not to untangle, and in this way, they are more content in the shadows. They have managed their affairs as to mostly avoid any genuine representational systems, or interactive ones, for they are both intricate in their regard, and instead opt to remain in localities and systems that espouse both in an incoherent and congruent manner.

For the representationally inclined, they are most unnerved by the shadow, for now they meet their own interactivity, which is extracted by the semblance of the representational aspect, but also does not sustain itself; thereby becoming the interactivity that is interlaced with the representational aspect. They cannot ignore the representational reality, nor can they disregard the interactivity that ascends by the fact that it is included within the representational imbuement.

This individuality or interactivity has now become unearthed, so that it is for them to deal with that ascendency. However, because the entire premise of this individualized interactivity made its way to the forefront because of representational activity or forms, all that privatization does date its lineage back to the perceptual form of the shadow, or the representational aspect contained by the shadow. If they approach such individualization through interactivity alone, they will enshrine the representational source of the individuality, so that in any direction, it would only strengthen that representation and thus lead to more privatization; in a never-ending loop of more detail of personhood, possibly more than is ever needed to attend.

Any direction of interactivity would lead to this predicament, whether one chooses to heal through traditional therapeutic mending or follows the details of that interactivity to its subconscious sources. First, mending does not avoid this, for the representational aspect becomes part of the process, only to renew the inclination toward interactivity through the reanimation of the perceptual form.

Second, if one follows the details of the interactivity in order to psychologically approach the subject, then despite whatever conclusion or development is reached, there will still incur a reanimation; due to the very validity of its proven lineage back to the representational aspect. This is why we often find that one's psychological state, despite the detailed availability of interactive liberties, is usually grounded in a singular representational form. It is that form which causes the ascendency, not the material itself.

Of course, one may continue to interact from a persistent reserve of individuality, sustained by the ongoing presence of the shadow within the psyche. It becomes a matter of preference: whether one chooses to deal with interactivity alone or the representational aspects alone; a concurrent separation is required.

The very loop of development is the cause of a rather downward spiral, because there is no separation of the shadow and its encompassing representational element from the privatization that ascends because of it. We can even account for this in a logical manner, where one recognizes that their interactivity, no matter the representational form, is inherently a personal matter. That there is a tremendous data stream of personalization that can be met for interactivity, and a representational element that charges for that ascendency is in no way connected to the interactivity.

The reason there is any lineage between the two is based on the manner in which shadows operate, whereby their interlacement of both interactivity and representational themes leads one unto their own interactivity; which is wholeheartedly separate. The shadow does not cause interactivity, just as a relationship's culmination does not cause the private experience of interactivity. It is merely because the relationship comprises both representational themes and interactivity, which, in its usual case, is noticed only for one or the other; and in its culmination, the wholeness of the relationship is noticed, eliciting the shadow and thus the perpetuation of individualized interactivity.

Whatever the process of dealing with that newfound experience of interactivity, as long as believed or extended toward the source of causation, it will only reanimate the entire process. Concurrently, one lives alongside a potent shadow, in which all ascendency of interactivity and procedure will reach into the representational form that is interlaced into the shadow.

For the example of a relationship, the only reason its potency dissipates over time is that the representational element loses its vibrancy, owed to both distance and "distance." One is physical distance, which is separated from performing as a representational element; the other is the case of proximation reactivated as separation, such that each encounter readily performs to decry the representational aspect, leaving only interactivity.

There is the case that the alternative occurs, whereas instead of the other party becoming more interactive, they develop to be more representational. Instead of their familiarity being based on the remaining relationship, each new encounter supposes a dissimilarity, albeit to engender a formidable representational element that is part of the fabric of general representations and does not comprise a singularity like a regular relationship.

Renowned and public relationships take this form, because the public recognition forces the element towards representational, and that private parties distinguish familiarity between themselves. It is both easier and more difficult when it is already ordained in a specific direction; for one to regulate the process but for the other to be a stronger participant in the representational aspects to which that may not be the normal choice of action.

The psyche's formalization of distance is what we are in discussion about, the one who distances the interactivity of their own regard from that of the relational theme, until, that is, they become wholeheartedly embedded in the process of personal interactivity. This occurs without animating the source, concurrently, there is no cause for more interactivity and the shadow has been lifted.

One does not need to access the interactive plane of their own psyche without the congruent measure of a perceptual form. Although we have discussed a shadow which elicits the possibility to transition into a liminal sphere of interactivity of one's psyche, it is not the only causation for access to one's subjective interactivity. One can access interactivity by following any perceptual form and identity a lack of synchronization, and in this way will gain access to their interactivity.

The first rule of any interactivity is that it requires a perceptual form, yet the first rule of perceptual forms is that it is not implicit with any interactivity because it is perceptual-based. It is only when some form of desynchronization occurs with the perceptual form that it gives access to one's subjective interactive base.

The quintessential example is the family body, which, like any other conceptual or physical sphere, relies on perceptual forms. But in the case of the family body, it contracts itself in order to subjugate that form so that it does not exemplify itself in its full modality. When viewed by both the perceptual form that gives credence to its construct and from its desynchronization and interpretation, one now has access to its internal interactivity so that a process of domestication can occur.

There are various methods for the perceptual form to lose its synchronicity, and we have mentioned the first, which is the shadow. Technically, one can identify the interactive elements of any perceptual form to gain access to its subjective interactivity, but in doing so, one is seeking the shadow elements already contained within the perceptual form; in the circumstance that one does not imbue oneself in that regard.

Any form of perceptual information can be constituted as a shadow, inasmuch as there is going to be some interactive element in its composition. However, the objective perspective of that composition constitutes whether it is a shadow or not, in that it naturally elicits a response in the subjective self toward compelled, involuntary interactivity.

One who resides by a garbage disposal would not constitute that experience as a shadow, and thus will not reflect upon their subjective self, although a bypasser will experience it as such. It is not because the garbage disposal is more shadowy or less shadowy, but rather because of the level of representational elements and interactivity that constitute the experience of that shadow.

Yet, there is the objective form that all would agree upon: the garbage disposal is both interactive and representational which elicits the formalization of a shadow. All the while, one can remove themselves from general sociality. This would be the case in the opposite direction, where one perceives what would objectively be considered representational and instead considers in a manner that is regarded as a shadow. A common occurrence of this is the perception of the affluent, whom the proletariat would view through all its interactive elements, despite it being representational at its core, and thus prove themselves to be beholding a shadow.

Despite the intention of this search being inauthentic, common sociality does not agree that the affluent is an interactive experience and rather views it as fairly representational; one would align with thát criterion. Yet it is upon regular sociality to conduct itself based on the concurrent ideation of what constitutes a shadow; that there is not an attempt to extract interactivity from a general consensus where there is none, or to claim representational in the case of interactivity.

The Integrated Shadow

Without an integrated shadow, where the individual or system, whether corporeal or otherwise, becomes exemplified by its intermediary contrast, another form will generate itself. This is because, without a contrast exemplified, there is going to be a found contrast, and if propelled to avoid the contrast, one beholds to become the contrast. This is because, whether by the alternative individual or alternative system, it will seek in what way it proceeds despite the nature of how it exists, and so long as there is an existential program in place, (the way it must adhere to a certain modality within nature) it will find itself to be regulated by its contrast. Such that we might say that as long as there is a pronounced program within reality, there will be two parts: that of the *thing* itself and that which contrasts the *thing* itself.

Many times, the very contrast is found in the attempt at being the *thing* itself, which is performed poorly and will then make itself pertinent as a shadow to the thing itself, exemplified by the inadequacy. The shadow will be found, not by the *thing* itself, but by the reality that was adhered by the *thing* itself, to which the contrast is made known. There is no *thing* without a contrast, and if we find such, it merely is not noticed that it is the contrast to another *thing* to which it follows.

This is the nature of an integrated shadow, where if there is no enemy, there is no friend; more so, there is no individual to which we can call an individual. The only way to find out the individual is through the background where the detail of 'non-individuality' is made known. The very degeneration of proposing the idea of liberty, for which, if there is no 'non-liberty,' we cannot be sure of the notion of liberty, for there is nothing to be liberated from. This is why populations may assume the role of war or conflict, for the very need to notice themselves as citizens is rather exemplified with its integrated shadow of conflict or the notion of its lack of permanence.

To raise the very preliminary question: in what way can we proceed to integrate a shadow, which will then approach becoming that very notion? For if we proceed upon conflict, then we are no longer the citizen or individual that exists on the other side of conflict; rather as though being a part of the conflicting apparatuses. Then the choice becomes paradoxical, for in the event of being undertaken by a shadow, in which one proceeds to liberate themselves, in the event of complete liberation, they are without the burden of the shadow and thus are not distinct in any manner of regard. They have left the arena of burden and one's definition of its realm, and need not become the liberated one but the undefined one.

This is why the very burden of the shadow is much needed to remain in some position, for when one reaches away from such a pronounced level, they lose all definition alongside that stroke of liberation. Yet, the very burden of the shadow is considered existentially burdensome, to a point that any notion that is not merged within the shadow is very difficult and usually not entertained. The child does not easily leave the shadow of their parent, or in the case of parents as the role of shadow, they do not leave in a generative form, because their definition and all existential leaning is through that participation.

Yet we must build a scenario wherein it is promising, in the case of liberation, to perform what we are terming integrated shadow, which does the work of including a newfound shadow. This is not to perform as any other function but being the shadow of that newfound process. Any corporeal system must adhere to this premise, or then be vulnerable to becoming themselves the shadow of some other thing. This occurs when one integrates a contrasting individual or system which is mediated without the complete appropriation of the individual. For if the individual or thing itself tends to the development of integrating the shadow, they become a part of that process, and as such are much the same in the shadow process. When one decides to enter into the utility of a system, the backend, the engineering aspects, they may be integrating that shadow, but also becoming a part of that shadow.

Yet without integration, where one sits above the utility of a process to be the 'thing' itself, they merely exemplify as such, since there is no adhesive correlation as peak persona or system when they do not participate in the integrated shadow. This is the in-between of the two extremes, where there is an appointment to the role of shadow, but without much integration, yet still with enough that can consider the shadow as true contrast of the *thing* itself rather than standalone engineering without contrasting correlation.

Without the integrated shadow, the existential program of the individual or system is then a very limited arena of space which is used as contrasting material to the broader scheme. This is why we cannot have the simple model of individual vs. world, or system vs. world, for the binary status has the weaker one, that of the individual or limited system, become a shadow or contrast of the better one; and in no event will the individual be a *thing* for which the 'world' is its contrast, and the same would be for any system or corporeal structure.

This is the reason for the three-model system, where there is individual and their integrated shadow, for the liberation of that shadow and onwards to the world. In this case, the 'world' cannot become the shadow of the individual, for they are already confined to a more limited sphere of control, and that limitation serves the individual from becoming a limitation of the broader scheme by having been burdened with a limitation. This is why young children do not become affected as would adults from societal consciousness (not individualist as would be pornography), because they are assumed to be under the conditions of their guardians, which in the very term of 'guard,' as being the shadow of the child. They are in limited function and will not become entrenched in societal proceedings.

However, in the case where the parent does not take the role of a shadow, where they are not viewed by the child as a confinement of personhood, as in the case of a dignified parent who does not limit or confine the child within guardianship, the child will proceed onward into society; as they are not beholden to a shadow against which they must contend in contrast to their individuality.

This very notion of a shadow for individuality has another ability to contrast the distinctness of the individual, such that they are confined by a personal contrast that exemplifies themselves as they *are* and have no ability to be something differing from themselves; for the contrast is customized to who they are. Without an individual shadow, they are not experiencing their contrast, and because of this, they are unavailable to the individuality and details of their distinctness, which, whatever their endeavor, will be imaginative, for they have no bearing of themselves as they *are* but only in what way they assume themselves to be.

Therefore, there is always going to be a distinction between the individual shadow and the system's shadow, in so much as an individual partakes in such. It is always the case that it leads back to individual participation, for if that is controlled, then a system without an integrated shadow would not affect them; more so, in the case of man overbearing shadow. It is only in the case of determinate participation that we begin the discussion of the system's shadow, but it is not so in the case of the individual's shadow. For in any case one is an individual of the broader environment and as such will be a determined system of their own.

In the case of an individual, we must first determine their existential landing in regards to relationships, and from there we can define their shadow process. Even if an individual avoids all relationships, there is a history of relationships, and in those, they are either to become the shadow or the *thing* itself; for which others are to become the shadow.

For example, if one is not with their childhood family, nor so with any newfound attachments, they do not contain a program of individuality and thus are automatically enclosed into the broader system from which they are another limited function of broader sociality or reality. They are akin to an abandoned storefront, to become both something of substance but limited to the streamability of social function. This is only in the case where the individual has another existential program from which to be 'an individual' for society, but when there is no such program, then they are without the need for being a shadow but still cannot be termed an *individual* in any sense.

However, such is very rare, and the individual will proceed to some level of relationship with individuals, or personalized aspects of structured reality; as in the case of insanity. Such will either determine them to be a contrast to that relationship or the *thing* from which the other side is contrast. When an individual has a personal shadow, their occurrence in broader reality will be regulated from the burdened arena of their private confinement. In the case where they remove or do not participate in an individual shadow, then they are at the mercy of sociality from which they can become the shadow, or rather a participant of that realm.

They become the shadow when they find themselves within an existential program within that reality. The only way to avoid such is to neglect to adhere to an existential program, or to do so without becoming the shadow of that program. This can be done by and through context, which controls and regulates the function of that participation, such that it will not be the articulation of them vs. the broader reality but as them in the regulation of that broader reality; where it is integrated and not represented. They are not considered individuals in that case but a bridge from their individuality towards this reality, where their modality of *being* is used to retract to the wholeness of their persona.

Although this may seem not to be the case, we need not look further than personnel that are part of a corporeal system, which, if functioning properly, will not be threatened from becoming a shadow of the environment. This is because they as individuals contain the context of the corporeal participation, and as such only serve as a bridge to that corporeal reality. An associate in store is not participating in that reality from an individualistic vantage point but rather as exemplified personnel for the corporeal function. The reason this works is because their psyche views corporeal process as but another context that reaches away from individuality. As such, we would not agree that an associate is a shadow of an environment even if we do not know the environment or the corporeal system; so long as the systems are functioning properly, they do not become the contrast to the environment.

Of course, the corporeal system itself can become a shadow of the environment, for they are serving that shadow and will partake in the contrast, but this is still from a contextual vantage and not the shadow itself. This is why, despite the white-collar crime of persons, they are not degenerate characters because they only performed the function of the corporeal system, albeit as a contrast to the good of society, and with such context, they have not integrated the shadow in full form. This is also why a judicial society does not treat corporate crimes with the same tenacity, for there are not persons of that organization that have beheld the complete contrast to society, but are only the organization as a whole, to which the judicial enactment will only proceed upon the organization, and the associates responsible are merely accounted for by setting an example.

This is the reason that corporeal systems are so promising to a functioning society, for they automatically offer context to the environment, and once the individual is integrated in that system, they cannot become a shadow of that environment. Yet, in the same token, the corporeal system can become a shadow like any system, but such is regulated by society and market exchanges. For the likelihood of continuing interaction with shadow systems will be slim and its degenerate pathway is inevitable. While in the case of an individual shadow, even if they are participating in a corporeal system, they may in fact proceed to utilize that context to lead back to their shadow origin. That is, in the case where the individual has become a shadow of the environment. In the case of a personal shadow, when they do participate with society through context, corporeal or otherwise, they do generate proceedings towards the individual aspect of being the shadow for other persons. This is how they can become enlarged in the very role of being the contrast, which, if reaching a pivotal moment, would have them become the thing itself with other persons becoming the newly elected shadow.

The change between roles occurs either internally or externally. We have just described a case of it occurring externally, where the development had enlarged the contrasting material to its pivotal moment. Or such occurs internally, wherein through a procedure of communication the contrasting side becomes increasingly frustrated with the tenacity of the subjects within confinement; noticing in how they have engineered a stronger system of contrast to something that does not regale in its proceedings. In that case, they begin to lose the availability of being at the role of a contrast since there is less justification, and now wither away from such a performance. Once they begin to fade away, they also reveal in what ways they are defined as something other than the shadow, and then it becomes the proceeding of the other persons to contrast such or to reveal a stronger sentiment.

PART TWO: THE CONCEPTUAL SHADOW

Conceptual Shadow and Sociability

Conceptual shadow is purposeful in its actualization much more than the material shadow, for concurrently, the genuine shadow, whether by perceptual realm or social extension through subjectification, is problematic from the onset as a proposition of true form, but only benefits in its manner of approach toward its distinctive differentiation.

As it were, a shadow is a disrupting force for streamlined consciousness or sequential process. Unless what is utilizing the shadow is doing so for its disrupting force, which is necessary at intervals, or for the purpose of finding its differentiated parts that would not be exemplified other than in the realm of the shadow. These include bygone elements that are propositional for current processes but do not fulfill the role of streamlined presentness, thereby the shadow providing such. It is the case that such a realm, in its functional process, not as a disruptive force but as an actualized realm, is of no significance.

This is not the case for the conceptual shadow, for it reflects not so much the immaterial aspect of consciousness but rather a sequential process of a conceptual framework that is looked upon from its differentiating standpoint, but more so in what way it fails to provide a sequential sequence. This is why the skeleton is the utmost shadow of the human form, because the human form, as a conceptual outlook, is performed. What is missing is its process of extension, especially in its intrinsic form, which is the beholden skeleton. It is an element of the conceptual outlook of the human form when looked at as a sort of corporal entity. This is missed by the skeleton aspect.

The reason it is necessary to approach the conceptual shadow against the behest of the corporal entity of the human form is because the corporal structure requires dissemination or dissolution in order to make way for an approach toward aspects that are more social. Because the conceptual framework is in itself a non-animated element; thus the corporate structure that defines the human form is simply a construct that helps with sociability. It requires its intrinsic dissolution in order to make way for the more social effects of the human form that are not pertaining to it, such as the skeleton, which is true in the intrinsic nature of the social aspects of human form that do not fit into the corporate structure.

Because of this, it is beneficial to approach the conceptual shadow only inasmuch as it disenfranchises the corporal structure, such that one is at a neutral state in attendance to the corporate structure of the human form, neglecting the more available social aspects. Or on the other side, the approach of the social aspects that are outside the corporate structure in and of itself. Thus, there is this intrinsic balance that is necessary in the actualization of the corporal shadow or the conceptual shadow, where it can go to the extreme, which is just as disruptive, where one believes the skeleton experience reflects merely the corporal structure that is meant to enter into social aspects only from itself; thus that the human being is somehow this experience of skeletal form and disrupting degeneration.

It is not meant as a conceptual shadow to perform in its specific state but rather to disenfranchise the corporate structure to allow for the openness of sociability yet not to have this social aspect become the new intrinsic human form. This is because such is not even a corporal structure in itself but rather the detail of a social aspect that cannot fit in the conceptual shadow.

On the other side, more may believe that one should avoid the conceptual shadow just like the material shadow and its functional form, because of the effect of building not only a disenfranchisement of sociability connected to the corporate structure, but also of a tendency to shadow elements in and of themselves; thus lost to many areas of consideration, that one would never enter the human form via the skeleton utilizing the conceptual structure in order to disrupt the human form and redefine such against general sociability.

With this in effect, one may view the actualization of the infrastructural shadow as too much of a disruption, when, in the other extreme, one believes the conceptual shadow to be true in its utmost state and thus becomes disillusioned from the sociability that it is meant to be in service of. Thus, the human form takes on such an extreme proportion that it is believed to be experienced as the true existential state, avoiding every aspect of sociability, whether of the shadow or of the general process of experience. This is because the experience of life as an exemplification of life is first and foremost a conceptual structure of what constitutes life, and thus its polar opposite is not necessarily the experience shadow in its material structure that defines life, nor necessarily the degeneration of the human capacity as an experience. In this way, the fear of death in that context will be in consideration of the conceptual shadow in regards to life and purposeful to allow for the experience of further life that is not disrupted by adherence to the conceptual formation of life.

Even in the case scenario of conceptual and material shadow, it can be layered upon a conceptual shadow, as in a dystopian reality, which is conciliatory, serving both as a disrupting force based on perceptual synchronization, but also as a conceptual shadow when we approach the subject of a dystopian reality in reference to civilization. The adherence to civilized elements themselves brings a forthcoming disparity when approaching the shadow in reality in reference to that.

Conceptual vs. Genuine Shadows

The difference between a conceptual shadow and a genuine shadow is merely in what way it attaches to a representation and the hierarchy of perceptual forms. In the case of a conceptual shadow, it is not the entanglement of a real experience of conscious examination to which it is delineated to a point where it consists of a shadow rather than to perform as the ideal, it is merely the conceptual platform that emanates from a starting point at a consciousness helm.

More so, it is a concept of consciousness rather than consciousness that is tangled with interactivity; no different than the other side of a genuine shadow, which is interactivity mixed with true representational activity. Although it is seemingly separate from the consciousness process and therefore cannot constitute any formation of consciousness or its shadow undertone, the concept is directly correlated and has a line that connects back to consciousness. This is especially true when it is considered a concept that stands on its own such that it proves itself as a conscious system in its own right; it will manifest as an experience of a conceptual shadow.

The difference between a conceptual shadow and a genuine shadow is that in the genuine shadow it is the persona or group and infrastructure itself that can only manifest such a shadow, because it is directly correlated to infrastructure and sociality. However, in the conceptual shadow, it is not merely the measurement of infrastructure; in fact, it is not reliant upon infrastructure or even sociality, but rather concepts or conceptual layout in mesh with interactivity. It is still reliant at some level with infrastructure and the perceptual system, but it is not the infrastructure that forbears the shadow department, but rather that it allows the concept to speak for itself.

Much like the marginalized suburb, in which it is less about the fact that it is an infrastructural locality, but rather that the infrastructure allows the concept and the value structure of what constitutes a suburban process, which then becomes entangled with interactivity, so that at no point is it considered a genuine shadow, and at most times it would be considered simple domestication or interactivity. However, it can be perceived, based on its concept entangled with interactivity, as being a conceptual shadow, especially in the cases where the concept is believed to be directly correlated to consciousness, or more so if the interactivity is stronger than the concept.

For instance, if one attempts to extract the higher level of interactivity in a suburban home more than its conceptual mainframe as a suburbia process, it will be experienced as a conceptual shadow, because it is attempting to formulate a stronger impression of the perceptual form such that the concept will require a stronger adherence. This would be as if it were a conscious system, such that its finality is to arrive at a conceptual shadow.

We have the process of constructing a conceptual shadow from either an overbearing interactivity unparalleled to the concept, or when the concept itself is believed to be a conscious structure in its own right, or if it is noticed as having direct lineage to consciousness, which is never its true effect, but can be experienced as such. Those who experience the conceptual shadow as such are going to be those same individuals who formulate the process of their psyche through conceptual mainframes, and believe that those concepts are the true nature of consciousness and reality. Such that now, when they enter into a sphere where there is both the concept and interactivity enmeshed as one, they are forced to differentiate and thus remain in a state of perpetual disparity until they admit the concept as a conscious structure is false, or that the concept is not the true nature of the entire possibility of conceptual ideals, or avoid the interactive aspects and continue being participants of the strong conceptual formula. As we notice, anything with very strong context will avoid any formation of intimacy, and thus will not have the possibility of differentiation by virtue of being purely theoretical in all of its experience.

Tragic Form and Discontinuity

The tragic form is the entrenchment of a corporal injunction or separatist experience that has no ability to reconfigure with its preliminary consciousness helm. This is why we can articulate the human condition to be tragic: because at some point or another one is detached from a conscious continuum, and in that way it can be viewed as tragic. That is, to identify the inability of conscious sequence, one needs to follow the complex articulation or the entrenchment to which one has resided and its inevitable unavailability toward resequencing to what it was a derivative of. This is why tragedy is usually associated with instant disenfranchisement rather than a slow and continual process, because in that way one moves too quickly to pay attention or extract in what way the derivative of that consciousness leads toward whatever new realm they are entering.

However, in an alternative to the tragic plunge, that realm is sequenced upon itself, such that if, in the ability of articulation from its internal database, it is more perfected than if it was connected to that which is beyond it. For in the connection, there is going to be an inability to gain access to the data process of an internal organization because it is dependent upon the way it is disconnected. However, this is also a tragic form, where one is more available to the data of its internal process in the tragic jurisdiction but without the ability of extracting it. The tragic form is dependent on a third-party to extract the data and thus formalize it as a purposeful stream to which it should connect to what is beyond it.

This is why tragedy in any art form is naturally purposeful: because it is reliant on the viewer, or the external third-party, who connects the tragic aspects to what is beyond it. But in the internalization of the tragic form, or in the subjective state of that tragedy, one is truly in the experience of tragedy, and thus without an ability to exemplify that in an art form. This is the major anomaly of any participation in tragic art form, in that it is already based on a supposition that is nonexistent in the subjective experience of such, being wholeheartedly dependent on the viewer. And in the realization or the removal of the viewer experience, one would not appreciate or answer via the art form, since that is simply the experience of a tragic form to which it is a natural inclination for one to avoid disturbing a conscious connection and entering a realm that is devoid of such.

This is not to say that the disconnection of consciousness between realms is not purposeful in itself, for in the opposite extreme of constant connection there is no believability of stabilization in data or in analysis, such that there is a requirement of disconnection; but not so much that there is a loss of recognition toward a consciousness helm. If one has lost all access and entered a complete depressive state, it has no remediation other than through a third-party action or third-party viewer.

PART THREE: THE SUBJECTIVE EXPERIENCE OF THE SHADOW

Entering the Shadow Locale

Seeing that the shadow is subjective first and foremost, we can approach any so-called objective shadow and reanimate it to the most significant preset for consciousness distribution. The reason for this is that the shadow enters via perception through the interactive projection rather than through social extension of that sentiment. Yet it is true to the nature of its perceptual representation, and it is only for one to enter through that recognition to produce the effect of its proper position within the scheme of non-shadow elements.

It is only considered the shadow as long as it changes to its subjective stance; much like the proletariat who jumps the position of their rather mediocre social class and presents themselves to be containing interactivity that is on par with what would be considered social extension. But rather, it is the fact that because they have entered through a simple interactive presentation, they are in effect becoming part of the shadow representation of the *thing* itself.

However, we can entertain the proletarian existence and recognize its rather deeming effect of what would be considered a purposeful intersection of the true nature of conscious dissemination; not from the vantage of its interactive standpoint, which is subjectively experienced as a shadow, but more so in what way it would service the full spectrum of the system.

It is true that every shadow element is merely the differentiation of a piece of consciousness, but it is only considered the shadow because it attempts to interact stronger than its proposition of differentiation. In fact, we could call the other category, or the third category, that of being external to the purview of a shadow; since it does not partake in any sort of differentiation. But by any definition of the shadow element, it has to participate at some level in the differentiation of conscious dissemination, only for the fact that it is propositioned stronger than its extension of social ascendancy. And most likely it is the case that it is pushing what has been bygone, presented and fallen from the purposeful representation of continuing dialogue; and in that way becomes a considerable shadow.

One can always reach back into the shadow element, or, in this particular case, the differentiation of a specific element of consciousness, and bring it forth. But it is usually the case that it will be presented as a performance, much like a glass casing that is surrounding the proletariat like an artifact, which displays and showcases what it would be like to be a proletariat and in what way they present themselves as tethered according to that relevance. In that case, it would be completely connected to its participation in the light of consciousness rather than its shadow; because it continues the concurrent dialogue.

But the matter of fact is that offering animation to a shadow element, or the showcasing of its specific relevance as a differentiated part (which so happens to be in degeneration and not deserving of its effect as a participating member to that degree) it would be the case that both are at a loss of regular availability towards consciousness (since there is good reason why it is declining as a differentiated part). More so, it is offering for the subjective stance of that specific shadow presentation a purposeful structure. This is besides offering conscious vitality for it to continue despite its degeneration. Almost as if it is offering life to what is meant to dissipate, and thus disruptive as a force not so much in the realm of consciousness, but more so as an enlargement or engorgement of the shadow element as a disrupting force; with stronger vitality since it is being offered a new chance of survival.

The problem with actualizing the shadow is not so much for the sake of its content business (since, as we noted, it is a true representation of a specific differentiation factor), but more so because it offers the animation to present itself stronger as an effect to the perceptual arena; more so to the social exchange. In both cases, this would be at the cost and behest of a stronger disturbance to the ability of the conscious process.

In the case of the former, where it upsets the perceptual realm, it is more so the expansion of the shadow realm as it pertains to perception. It is more likely the case that there is going to be an expansion of the physical elements and structural presentation of those particulars of the shadow, thus enabling what we termed the shadow locale.

The social adherence based on a subjectification of the shadow elements, to the point where one simply needs to enter that space to experience the presentation of a shadow, is much like the apocalyptic experience of entering a rundown location where the population has plummeted. All its perceptual elements present themselves not as social relations but rather as differentiations that do not meet the behest of that social extension, and thus to experience the shadow locale.

In the case of an actualization of the shadow locale, in contrast to this objectification of the original shadow based on a social element, it is going to act differently; since it is already in the perceptual realm. If one enters a dystopian locale of the aforementioned and brings the social aspects pertaining to a connection to consciousness or is of the belief that consciousness continues, one of two things may happen:

1. The shadow, in this case, the dystopian system, will exemplify itself as elements of particulars pertaining to its relation to conscious dissemination. This will showcase it as a dystopian locale "in reference to consciousness," thus reanimating the dystopian system as alt-dystopian yet perfected within the realm of a neutral state showcased of its differentiation. This is why a dystopian film or book is purposeful, to experience additional sentiment of civilization rather than complete abhorrence to it; because it is viewed through the lens of its differentiating elements. As though now we can enter via this portal that suspends civilization and focuses on very specific particulars that make up this civilization. That is a narrative trick, to enter those rooms which in the regular case would not be possible.

2. However, the more usual scenario, and one that would be more existentially true, is not through that lens, but in actuality, the articulation of that dystopian experience as

though it is at the behest of itself. Therefore, all prior civilizational tendencies fall, and that becomes the true realm; much like what would be the experience of the character within that dystopian state, which is not noticed when it is articulated through a narrative frame.

Such a character would experience the perceptual realm of that experience in how those specific elements which make up this shadow locale do not connect under any purposeful agenda; it is merely the scattering pieces of civilization. Therefore, there will be the animation of those particulars in their adjacent disruptions. Because there is a memory of civilization afforded to each one of these characters, it is not experienced as a newfound state of experience; where they are simply scattering parts that make up no specific whole, nor specific in each of their parts. Such a memory would be at the behest of the wholeness that is behind this differentiation, which thus will animate itself as a shadow locale; but in reference to the character as an experience of the existential shadow. This will disrupt any sort of sequence in their mind in lieu of these scattered elements of non-adjacent connections.

For the individual, they now become part of the shadow and experience individuality from this vantage point. Such an individual will know, after the fact, external from this locale, particular elements that are bygone of the social streamline status of concurrent consciousness, and will focus on those elements in particular to find residency in such. Always on the lookout for expressive interactivity, whether materiality, whether locale, or social aspects, that are thus representing interactivity in an exorbitant level that presents itself as the dissipation of concurrent consciousness. It is those things that are set in stone in their interaction with reality, always experiencing anything concurrent or less interactive, and thus particular to the streamlined social process. And in its stead, they become focused in what ways there is a failure of final distribution of specific aspects or things, and in this way, they continue the lineage of the shadow in whatever they interact with.

Such an individual can either begin their process through the focus of this objectification in a perceptual form of the conscious shadow, or they can actualize in the realm of the shadow locale and thus continue throughout their goings and comings.

In the first case, of the subjectification, they are simply presenting interactivity at a stronger sense than the perceptual realm agrees, and thus begin their day in accordance with the perceptual realm. But it is they who have begun the initial process of creating the shadow locale from the vantage of their social subjectification. They are bred and wired to orient themselves toward interactivity against the perceptual realm, and thus become accustomed not only to the shadow locale when it finally presents itself in perceptual form, but also in whatever interactions they take upon themselves at any period of life.

It may be at the later stage of life that they have gained through the shadow, by following a level of intellectuality, otherwise known as wisdom, and the particulars of the details of that shadow rise above the shadow, but still pertain to being particular to the shadow since they have the ability to articulate its specific differentiation.

It is in this manner that any dealings with the shadow become successful, when one has an intellectual lineage toward the shadow so that any of its differentiated parts are not actualized for itself or how it presents itself through its objectification, but merely in what way it can be conducive to the perfection of whatever intellectual lineage has been used to participate with these elements. Chief among them is noticing the reason such material elements or aspects have fallen to the role of shadow, and in how they reflect back to what it was previous to its shadow form.

In the other case, in which one actualizes the shadow locale but previously was not such, like in the way one enters into a dystopian realm in the case that they were previously existent in a civilized system, it is only after the fact, when they depart from this shadow locale that they continue that way of processing thought material. The fact that they perceive interactive elements of the perceptual realm specific to the ones that are not streamlined to social extensions, are thrown into disruptions between each thought because of their disability, and have actualized any realm that is without sequence, and specifically is anti-sequence.

Thus, whatever realm they enter, they perceive or ignore sequence and instead favor disruptions between thoughts, retaining only enough continuity for each to intersect with the perceptual realm.

This is the more dramatic case: one bred in the shadow is acclimated, while one who enters it unknowingly loses their bearings and suffers loss in sequential thought, perception, and social ascendancy. More so, they have no effect in the details of their shadow realm because they believe it to be the true nature of experience, such that they do not utilize an intellectual tradition to find differentiation between its parts.

This is why intellectuality is paramount, for even if one actualized and thus continues onward in whatever dealings, by following an intellectual tradition they will begin to find sequence once again; and disrupt the idea of disruptive sequence, or that interactivity has no bearing on other interactivity. Just as intellectuality restores sequence and navigates the shadowed interactivity, we must consider the underlying structures, the infrastructural realms, which set the parameters within which social and perceptual elements may or may not align.

Infrastructural Realms and the Limits of Social Integration

The infrastructural realm, and by that, we mean anything that pertains to the base exemplification of structural reality that does not consider the social layer projected upon it, is positioned against the integration of sociality because it is strictly defined as something that does not understand or correlate with sociality; it is infrastructural and distinctive. The distinct characteristic of an infrastructural realm is based on its structural parameters and its relation to other structural connections or disconnections.

For example, a bus is a form of public transport, because it is irrespective of sociality that allows it to be a correlated spatial arena. The arena is separated by sociality for the fact that it bridges structural connections, which cannot be said for an isolated room. It is not due to the fact that it is public as opposed to private, but rather that it maintains structural adherence between locations.

The social imprint upon the structural realm is based on the consideration of locations in respect to other locations, but all remain defiantly correlated to infrastructural realms. Such that, if there is a gated separation, despite social interests in regard to the gated realm, it will not correlate because there is a structural separation.

We understand that there is a near-infinite number of dynamic inferences between the two realms, although they're distinctly separate from each other and have no intrinsic correlation other than social relevance, which then again translates to infrastructural change.

Existential Ground and the Mediation of Disparity

In the stasis of an existential aspect, defined by parameters given to things associated with identity-relationships across other modalities toward reality, develops into an existential ground which is akin to a specific locality. This serves both to organize itself and, in its manner and orientation, to define what lies beyond.

As is the case of a locality that contains any existential or social meaning, there will be a buffer between locations, such as a state of existential standing in which what lies beyond it is defined by the disparity between itself and what it cannot function as. Because of this, the political layer, or, in the case of the psyche, the superego intervenes as the separating element with regard to existential standing.

In this way, when one senses existential disruption, that conservatory element separates their existential standing from what lies beyond. Thus, politics, or its notion as a social function, is merely the simplification of the disparity between one existential standing and another. The act of entrenchment within that disparity is the unwillingness to disrupt the threatened existential ground, or to make way for newly emergent existential territory, such that the encounter itself establishes the disparity that separates it from its broader reality.

Dread, Duality, and Social Becoming

One does not extend within that social aspect, because there is no social aspect within the corporal structure, and thus one has taken defensive positions to exclude themselves from even enjoining in the game that is to become part of the social extension and outside the influence of the shadow elements. We find this very common as a Victorian heritage: the well-to-do will perform such a function in that they begin to avoid socialization, and especially the shadow elements, for they presume that what is necessary is to be beyond the shadow to partake in any social development. But at the same time, they become part of a corporal system that is the well-to-do class or such, and in that case become corporal in its entirety and thus external to all socialization.

Thus, you have the common theme of the Victorian personality that has no real knowledge of what is socially prevalent even at an existential level. In that same way, in the protective realm outside any matter of consequence, and thus in their defense of the shadow elements, indeed they become unavailable to any influence or existential development. Thus we have before us the constant ascension toward corporal structures in order to be distant from shadow elements, but in doing so, without an able body to partake in social extension.

The reason for the difficulty in avoiding both the shadow elements and partaking in social extension is that one cannot ignore the shadow elements, for they are part and parcel of general socialization. But at the same time, one must partake away from that element, or at least in its actualization, such that one must live a sort of duality. Such duality is hard to come by because one must recognize and at least include the shadow elements, or at least their availability, that they move away from, in order to enter general socialization. And thus it is only available to one who is conceptually inclined toward both elements. For if they actualize in the shadow realm, they have not the ability to proceed beyond that, because they have become such, like their counterparts; and if they avoid such in a systematic manner, they have simply created a corporal structure, as the Victorian heritage has done.

Thus, the only possible way is to avoid permanence within the shadow realm but include its elements as though a research study or a detailed analysis through conceptual overlay, with this inclusion toward the extension, that is, when they do reach social competency and thus either actualize or at least process the subject with a higher degree of intimacy.

The other possibility in dealing with the shadow is to name it as its namesake, and thus partake in the effect that it is a shadow, and thus recall one's personhood within such a realm; to differentiate and decompose, populating itself as would any shadow that overrides the wholesomeness of a human endeavor. In other terms, the shadow experience, as one who walks late at night and experiences dread, is not only allowed but is sought after, such that they become decomposed, populated, and enabled in their existential grounds, and thus move about within such a realm in whatever way they see fit.

It would seem that it is almost an anomaly that this approach has not been taken seriously throughout the heritage of dealing with the shadow, in which it is simply the case that one need participate in the dread of such, disallowing the wholesomeness of socialization but still partaking in its differentiation as it breaks down in the face of the shadow, and thus able to enter via the existential dealings which, in any case, are important to the construction and process for the eventual wholesomeness of general sociality and extension.

This wholesomeness has anyway the requirement of differentiating itself at one point or another, whether through domestication or intellectual compartmentalization; that the shadow is just another offering to decompose that wholesomeness in a way where one experiences their existential dread of those backhanded aspects, and can be viewed as a differentiation through decomposition and as thorough and purposeful as an agenda for human endeavor.

We may have one reason why such has not been the approach, for such dread has been generally viewed as though biologically threatening, as though it would be to experience crime or other factors that give way to the elements of the shadow, and in this way become viewed as not only simplistic existential decompositions but biological disruptions and possibly the degeneration of human existence and its actuality. In this way, it is viewed as just another case of biological protection and unapproached as a scenario of experience.

This is a common misconception in regard to all existential dread, which is generally viewed as its near cousin, that of biological threat, and in this way becomes coupled in its view of automatically avoiding its onset and doing everything in one's power to protect oneself from that experience.

This is a terrible mistake, for in that case one has no access to their existential state, more so, they have no ability to experience the whole purpose of the shadow in its raw state, and instead become actualized as the shadow, as though they have become the *devil* for another individual rather than experiencing the dread of simply being under the auspices of the *devil*, in lieu of the next stage of becoming wholesome once again.

What becomes of all this is the contemporary degeneration of most developed countries, being of corporal structure through governance and social assumptions, and in this way the only access to socialization is the degenerate parts of that society, or the downtrodden places that avoid interacting with the regular state of human affairs. But in that way, they are the only members of true socialization in that entire statehood and thus are primary in any further process, and serve as the social bridge toward whatever corporal structure continues onward.

Thus, the most crime-ridden and degenerate populace is the leadership of the entire state in its attempt to remove its shadow elements. If one would simply want to access socialization of any state, they must go to where there is less governance, less corporal structure, and in that way they have entered not only socialization but the worst of its kind, which has not been able to be integrated into the corporate structure, therefore the very detrimental social body; but in that way they are the only members of true socialization of that system.

It is as though the dreadful late-night experiences are the only element of any social regard, and all other corporal structures that awaken at dawn to participate in what would seem like judicial, state-like experiences is simply the bridge through which the social degeneration is now articulated for the next day forward.

This is the cause of strong governance and the removal of the shadow, allowing it to function as a corporate structure, along with the agreement of populists and citizens to avoid the detestable experiences associated with shadow elements entering a social organization. Consequently, the outside realm is not even considered external but is seen as additional corporate procedures, which one has never truly encountered through socialization, whether individually or through familial experience.

Limits of Perception

The shadow locale will be exemplified in a more infrastructural form when it reflects peak consciousness, but will do so in a more conceptual format when far from it. This is because the shadow exists as a reflection of consciousness, so that if consciousness is of a kind that is conceptual and only permits a portal into its real form through conceptual realization, then the shadow will be conceptual and less dramatic from a biological presence. This is the horrific imagination that succumbs to itself; for instance, the dread of insanity is a regular symptom of this conceptual shadow, while at peak reflection it appears more as a material threat. This dread is never realistic, for if it were, it would be regular violence, neither shadow nor consciousness.

We could view this through the perspective of trauma, which can only occur in the shadow. If it were the experience of consciousness, then it would be a revealed element of consciousness to the nth degree, but would not be imprinted against the process of sequential patterns within the psyche. Yet, when there is an experience of the shadow of consciousness, which systematically reflects against its prevalence, one will not be exposed to consciousness per se, but will not shy away from it. Thus, the threat is both existent and nonexistent, and this is the format for trauma. The less connected the experience is from its revealed expectation of what it is, the more it can be considered as performing as a shadow; thus being both connected and disconnected, leaving one lost to a direct and sequential direction to and fro that experience.

The highest degree of trauma is the greatest expectation of devastation with the least actual damage, considering that it still evokes an emotional response due to a certain alignment. If the expectation of dread is lessened, or if there is damage of considerable nature in proportion to the expectation, or if there is no sign that has the psyche believe that devastation is forthcoming, then the trauma will be mitigated.

In this manner we can view the shadow, for its highest prevalence being most recognizable to consciousness with the least amount of signage to make consciousness possible. This would be the greatest format of the shadow. If, for instance, the prevalence of possibility of consciousness is not forthcoming, or if there is no performance that can be presumed to enter into consciousness while still not entering, then the shadow will be weakened. Additionally, when the dread or experience of loss is too strong, it loses its reflective properties and rather becomes melancholia or grief, a symptom of a loss of consciousness instead of being a measure of the equation.

Shadow of Ascendancy

Dependency of the shadow pertains to the way it affirms itself by counteracting interactive elements, creating a contrast to streamline sociability. This occurs in the event of a lack of success or suspension of streamlined sociality, where the shadow profiles itself at the base of a verifiable lack of identity or vitality to confront the reality constructed for itself.

The bygone elements or the background constitution to streamline sociability exist only when that sociability concurs and enables reflection. But in the case that it does not proceed accordingly, the shadow is left to either seek a deeper entrenchment in itself, that is, to work in double time to appeal elements of sociability to the point that it is forced into contrast. It finds itself perfected to perform at any level of a shadow organization, for if there is any existent sociability, there will be a certain amount of reflection of the shadow.

In the regular case, it is simply the prevalence of an existing distinction that has the individual proclaim and eventualize toward the shadow. But in this case, it is the active seeking of the shadow elements to become such; that is, to find in any case or circumstance the provision of a shadow, meaning there is adherence to the shadow as a construct rather than as a reflection of something greater.

The other case is in which the individual provisioning the shadow finds themselves with less reflective sociability to disillusion their shadow contraction: and either partakes in the little sociability available to them or faces an identity change by finding themselves unregulated in their formation of reality.

We can see this by way of an example: an immigrant parent or an indigenous parent who provides for the child all the new world's perfections. This becomes the shadow of the child, ready to do all in all to provide the life they imagine for that child. In this case, they have elected themselves as being the shadow of the child, which in itself is honorary and possibly prosperous if only the child is successful. But in the case where the child finds themselves less a part of that ascendancy, the parent finds themselves even more without standing, since they do not find whatever shadow elements they have embodied to be reflected or received in the child's success.

In this case, either the parent can take a stronger stance, by the elements that gear toward the shadow; to become better, to work itself again into the life of the child in the hope that at some point or another, some exemplification of light or success of social ascendancy would take flight, or the parent finds themselves disillusioned, since the very motive of the shadow has not been successful in its reflection or in receiving a reflection. Thus, they must face the enlargement of whatever reality comes before them, which becomes an identity disruption.

The very terminology of parents whose children leave home—"empty nesters"—reflects this. Their entire identity has been lost, since they were in fact nesters, or more so, the background to the ascent of their child, who has now completed their ascendancy, or at least reached a point where the parent no longer takes part in the parental dynamic. Now the parent is lost both to the domestic space—since it serves no one—and to the authority of identity, since they had given themselves to being part of the shadow in lieu of social exchange.

This is only the case where the parental choice was to be the provision behind the child's ascendancy, which is not always necessary. It is possible that the parental process need not take part as the shadow, as we can see in the educational system, which bears much of the responsibility for the child's education, thus granting the parent the right not to become the shadow of the child.

It seems likely that the point of responsibility is upon the shadow, since it is either the case that one needs to move away from shadow elements, because they do not pertain to a natural point of reception to a reflective aspect of sociability, or move closer into the depths of the shadow, thus defining a profession of the shadow in any event or circumstance.

We often find this with parents who have become so entrenched in the child's ascendancy that they have focused only on the disruptive elements of the child, to the point that it creates irritation, disruption, and anger in every dynamic with the child. This happens because they have committed themselves to continuing unabated toward being the shadow of the child, and thus finds themselves, after the child's failure to gain ascendancy, irritated by the very shadow elements of their own persona which exemplify the ways they have failed to achieve that social ascent. Moreover, it appears as though the entire family unit is merely a shadow to some other social ascendancy, and thus the parent's sacrifice is rendered without meaning, at least within the family unit, though at some point it reaches toward a broader social ascendancy, since a shadow cannot exist without its reflective surface.

It might seem that it is the child who has failed in social ascendancy, yet we must also recognize that the development or affordance of social ascendancy can be a failure of systemic proportion, involving aspects outside the control of either child or parent. In that case, it becomes merely the realization that one is not prospering for their family unit, for the entire construction of that unit is at the base of a greater social ascendancy, especially in cases where streamlined sociability is not at its foremost ability, to the point that there is only simple residency to the existence of that entire family unit, anchored by the parent to the child.

The choice, then, may not be to fall into the depths of the shadow, but rather to let go of that provision; to accept the sociability and existence of the parental and spiritual role, and to allow the child to fall into whatever place society allows them to be embedded. In that case, despite a lack of greater social ascendancy, there remains some existent ascendancy or participation, which then proves to be furthered in the wholeness of streamlined sociability in a universal sense.

The notion that there is some plateau or peak of social ascendancy to which all are in service is merely a fantasy, or more so, an example we can use to understand the process rather than the reality of the structure. For example, a political echelon is simply an intrinsic construction separate from sociability, representing a complete sacrifice of individuality and participation with society to the role of being a representation of society. Thus, even at the highest levels of government, there is less participation in sociability than among the proletariat.

On the contrary, when there is neglect to take a step toward the provision of social ability, meaning to garnish away from experience and participation in the shadow; all social participation occurs at the slowest interaction point, since there is no social engineering. It exists only later, behind the process of social participation.

This is almost like a car's construction without design or engineering having to take part: without a shadow, but also without an introduction to sociability. And it is not the shadow itself that engineers sociability, but rather the apparatus that makes for any form of sociability. As we know, most often one enters via the shadow because they want to participate at a level beyond what is available to them, thereby becoming the shadow, not for participation, but for an overbearing exuberance of dissipation.

This exemplifies a reflection point rather than sociality itself. It is a reflection point of being overbearing on the organic ascendancy of that social point, such that one acting as though they are affluent is a shadow of true affluence. They perform toward that social juncture without concern for its organic process within the scheme of things, becoming exemplifications of how this is contrasted with that order and its backward channel, as though they are showcasing how affluence negatively attributes an individual. As a picture painted or a performance: "Look at me, notice how I have lost all that surrounds the notion of affluence in order to ascertain toward affluence; notice at what expense all of this costs." Rather than what they foremost believe, that this is in and of itself an excellent experience.

As would be the case of the child to whom the parent adheres in their development within social ascendancy, it can either be that the child views the parental apparatus through the lens of parental neglect of their persona, and thus a disregard for both the shadow's degeneration and its orientation toward the ability of ascendancy; or, in a less likely case, the child fuses the parent as the laden engineering behind what would be a better form of social ascendancy. But this ignores the notion of its inherence and thus its securing of the shadow to make way for the ability to approach social ascendancy at a higher level, for such adherence grants that right.

It is akin to equating a powerful engine with its engineering, yet not entering under the hood to become part of that notion through its shadow elements. This is done while still acknowledging that it exists to make for a case of social ascendancy greater than would be possible without the entire process of interaction with the vehicle.

In the extreme case of complete lack of notice of the engineering, which is less likely, as the market brings that notion by the cost of labor afforded toward such engineering, it would be without social ascendancy; or, at the other extreme, one may revere the engineering with admiration to the point of entering its realm hood and becoming part of that detail. They begin to take part in the shadow, or the apparatus, to the very social ascendancy which it is meant to provide, and thus become another member of the shadow to social ascendancy.

This is the general critique of Steinbeck in *The Grapes of Wrath*, where he dispossesses the notion of the affluent due to their lack of knowledge behind the engineering that underlies their vehicle; which, in that narrative, is of paramount importance. In actuality, it is a critique of becoming the very thing one must not take part in, for if they enter via the engineering at that level, they become just another number in the process of engineering toward a shadow that is meant to provide social ascendancy. This is not possible, as to be existentially behind the wheel yet within the very engineering that allows the wheel to function. It is very much a critique from the vantage point of the shadow, or more precisely, from the standing of the shadow viewing the affluent with disdain for their lack of participation in the engineering, assuming that in no case should one partake in social ascendancy, but rather should remain within the engineering that provides for it; more so within the self-debasement as being a shadow to social ascendancy. One does not agree to such a standing and instead finds favor in those who proficiently exhibit such ascension, as though they are the expense for the affluence.

A critique from the vantage point of a shadow is never considered a critique, since it is simply the exemplification of a shadow rather than participation in what social ascendancy entails. Once we ignore the expense ratio of that shadow, we begin to understand. However, it remains the case that there are social aspects noticed within the shadow that pertain to a degeneration of social ascendancy, but these are in no way reflections of the wholeness of that ascendancy; merely inference points that may or may not be of general regard. As would be the case of the affluent behind the wheel, it would be with much grievance of social ascendancy to take part in the engineering, and they would be deficient of a pathway toward understanding or developing their social ascendancy.

The one mention of such a critique is that it may be beneficial for the affluent to take part in the engineering at another interval, where they have background knowledge or have ascended from the vantage of the shadow and moved beyond it to social ascendancy. But in the case where they finally reach behind the wheel of the vehicle, it is in no way beneficial for them to take part in the generic engineering that lies behind it, for one cannot both participate in the shadow and attain social ascendancy without the expense of one or the other.

Shadow Persona

The Shadow as Performance: On Denigration, Representation, and the Loss of the Private

The shadow as an embodied persona will cause the individual, or perception of the individual, to be denigrated to the extent that it becomes possible to house the shadow. This is part of the practical implication of the shadow, whereas, because it embeds representational elements with individualistic ones, to which one is bound to the other, the individual who is private and excluded from the representational element will necessarily be denigrated. The partial element which is individualistic that takes part in the shadow is not the expression of the individual, even if individualistic.

There is an extraction process, which first identifies the private aspects and, instead of following their natural sequence of identification and expression, takes the element captive, all the while seeking a representational theme which can participate in that unification. The aspects which are connected to privatization are excluded from the amalgamation because they do not work with a representational element. Only that which sounds the part of an individualistic setting, one which can be performed to the representational element will be included. In the final outcome one has denigrated the genuine connection between the privation of the material and the shadow; which is experienced as self-denigration or self-hatred.

To illustrate, if one is naked and enters the public, they will concede to becoming a shadow, both for the structural environment and their persona, unless they somehow separate themselves from the social reality. Either through their acceptance or complete disengagement, like that of a muse or a deranged individual. The psychological activity that makes up this shadow is composed of two elements: namely, nakedness as it pertains to one's connection to selfhood and its privation, and the performative element of nakedness as it pertains to public exemplification. To be naked to the public, one must lose their connection to the privation of their nakedness, so much so that it becomes permissible to connect to the public performance of it. The final outcome has one denigrating their nakedness, or more precisely, the connection of their privation towards their body in the connotation of nakedness; in order to make room for the representational theme of public nakedness. There will be an automatic self-hatred that would be supplementary to the activity, in which one despises the private connections because they were forfeited for the benefit of the performance aspect. Such self-denigration occurs only after the fact, when the performance of the shadow has been engaged, because part of its process is its denigration.

It would be fair to term the shadow as a performance, since it always requires a representational theme, which is imbued with a private aspect. The definition of a performance in this context is the same: if it were only representational, it would constitute merely a perception of representation, but when added with the individualistic aspect, it becomes a performance of private themes contained by the representational aspect. The question then becomes: is all performance a shadow, or does it only work the other way?

Let us take stage acting, which includes both the representational aspects that corroborate with the public or audience, and the individualistic development that is imbued within the parameters of the play. Yet, we find that we separate the personage to avoid the subjective experience of the shadow, so that the actor is not the one containing the individualistic or private elements, and the writer/director is not the one corroborating with the representational aspect. Having them separated protects all personage of the stage play. Let us view the audience, which also finds themselves protected because they are fully in participation of the representational aspect, being that it is a public experience. Still, the performance itself is determined as a shadow, which could be termed in the theater industry as a mechanism that performs as a shadow but alleviated by separation of personage.

We notice this in governance as well, wherein those who provide executive decisions are separated from those in the realm of activity. The activity is performed wholly as a representational aspect, having very little connection to the private development that led to those choices of action. All the while, executives are devoid of all activity, having no realization or actuation of that end of the spectrum, which can then enter into a private accounting of the system of affairs and imbue it with coherent choice. This is why the killing of a leader is so catastrophic for a political institution: because they embody the private affairs that lead to the later activity in its representational format. When removed, it leaves a vacuum of representational activity without its private development.

The shadow is the case where, personally or structurally, there is no abiding by the separation; it embeds both in the same package. The reason for avoidance by any organization is because there is little consideration for both sides when the process of amalgamation is underway. One cannot adhere to both sides when an amalgamation occurs, and any aspect from either side will be staved off to perform the final shadow. For example, if the executive performed the activity, they would need to lose their overarching perspective in order to enter this liminal arena. All the while, they would need to depreciate the orderly conduct of activity, which has no learning of its preceding developments that led to this activity.

Thereby, they would be a poor version of either side, lacking in executive oversight and ordered conduct, such that they would not even have the subjective choice within the final performance; for some of the executive aspects will be staved off including the orderly ones, with no clear demarcation of what is what.

Relational Denigration and the Shadow Persona

A shadow persona does not view themselves as singular, but as part of an ecosystem. Because their individuality is tainted or denigrated, they do not gain vitality amongst themselves, and await the participation of that external ecosystem to animate their psychological state. In their relationships, the other proponent is perceived as part of the ecosystem to which they adhere, so that they are naturally dependent upon them, not in a manner of individual accession, but in the view of them as constituents of that ecosystem.

In general, they will not coincide with relationships that are outside that ecosystem, but more so will be highly attentive to the way the proponent is performing as part of that ecosystem. They do not engage with their individuality, or with the general definition of a relationship which relates back to the individual. They do not 'relate' to anything, for their 'self' is denigrated, without the composition to be related to. When it is proposed to relate to themselves, it is only in the aspect of denigration, so that in the final outcome, any experience of a relationship is realized as the manifestation of that very modality of self-denigration; which is the only manner in which they relate to themselves or any other person. They will either experience the manifest outcome of self-denigration, or project selfhood upon the proponent. This would denigrate them in the afforded manner by which they understand all relational procedures.

We are then misusing the word "relationship," for a shadow persona cannot manifest a relationship unless it relates to self-denigration. In the usual terms of their relationships, it is rather proponents who assist in fulfilling that representational element for the objective of their continuity as a shadow. Or else, they are alternative shadow personas which fulfill the ecosystem from which they extract to perform their continuing shadow. They view them as performances to which they can gain accession in their own performance. They can have an attachment to personas that wholly represent the environment because they do require the attunement of all things representational.

They are codependent only when there is misalignment with their attachment to the shadow persona. When engaged properly, there is no codependence, only inasmuch as it serves the definition of that ecosystem. When there is a slight detachment, one relates back to the self-denigrating part; and to the supplementary relational material which is individualistic. In that case, one relies completely on the other proponent to ensure that self-denigration is not sincere. To this effect, we have an individual who is self-denigrating, but then reliant on the other to ensure that such is not really the case. They are the safe keeper of the true individuality that lies behind that denigration. The only way to alleviate this is by removing the shadow persona, to which one now relates through a variety of individualized experiences.

The Shadow of Social Relationships: The Paradox of Center and Contrast in Personal and Collective Identity

The shadow is also necessary in personal affairs, as it were with the locale, it has a parallel domain for social relationships. We have exemplified that the shadow is found in the relatives of parental figures, for they are the center of the dynamic, and the others are existent to inform. They are not the shadows but more so the interactive units to differentiate the wholesome information of the parental figures themselves and their embodiment.

We find the shadow in relationships to the parental figure that do not inform directly but are an alternative approach that does not concern with the source. This is all in the perspective of the individual, for instead of it being an informant, it becomes an alternative distraction, so that the source, the parental figure is not being enlarged but being replaced. As it would in a shadow locale, it stops being an informational outlook of the center yet postulates itself against the source as the opposite. There is no alternative, existentially speaking, for the source is the only matter of concern, and any other version is always the opposite of its contrast, not the source itself.

The relatives of the parental figure will provide an alternative, yet it does not stand on fair ground because, in the perspective of the child, they are the opposite and contrasting, even if bearing a more complex version. One can task the parental figure for their lapse in the better version, but only through the figure themselves can the inquiry be had. Similarly, the shadow locale offers the contrast which allows one to reenter the center locale to find reason in the choices of its version, despite the resolution that there should not be a case where there is a departure from that source.

We have used the parental figure as the prime social example, because being the center for the child is intrinsically bound, whereas in other socialities the center can deviate. However, this depends on the initial impression of the center figure of sociality. If, in the case where that is found to be less effective, the informant figures, or those who postulate a shadow, will undo the fabric of the center until an available choice can be made to perform a genuine replacement; either upgrading the shadow or the informant figure.

Yet, we must know that as long as there is an existential impression of the initial center, any attempt at replacement will only extenuate the problem. This is the usual justification for a shadow locale or interactive one, by promising to upend and replace the center system, which is far superior and complex; that the attempt becomes a seclusion and detachment from the source of one's vitality. We notice this is in full effect when one attempts the replacement of the parental figure with others, only to become more entrenched in the elements that lose sense of the viability in which they are being provided. The shadow will remain such, only becoming more enlarged with more resentment at the cause of distance from the source.

As with Plato's analogy, there is always a shadow to a more complete light, and this, if found in sociality, a shadow can exist for being the possible replacement when we consider all the aspects of the *light* to which it informs and loses vitality from, not because we have not explored all vantage points but due to its frailty as a substance of influence and our interaction with it. We become integrated with the prior center, so much so that we do not find anything stimulating with a reencounter with its premise. Influence wanes for one of two things: either it was not a force of nature, only impacting at a surface level, or one engages with the influence to such a degree that it no longer has anything to say. There is always the possibility of re-actualization, because influence is not a thing in itself but a result of actualization.

For instance, the halted elevator creates a circumstance of actualization. We would not say it to be of a specific influence parameter, but due to actualization, the engagements are impressionable. When influence wanes, it is available for re-actualization. By the convergence of systems or sociality, one begins from square one by making them a center. However, it may be the case that one does not require the influence of this character, for being an influence that is not necessary. We usually actualize social relationships based on a need for that influence, which has one require that impression. What is possible, moreover, is that the actualization had simply come about through other methods, methods which one should care very much to avoid, and one is bound to center themselves with that dynamic.

If one actualizes a shadow, say for instance of a parental figure, then they have performed the deed of their attachment to the parental figure and their source of vitality. Even the parental figure may be possible as an actualization that would have one's post-childhood relationship take to the background due to the convergence of that source. This is why the source itself can cause the same, if not more, damage. When they are believed to be the only source, that it is the peak of existence, when in fact they are one of many sources within an elaborate set of psyche impressions, then all others fade away.

Similar to how the center locale, even the center of civilization cannot be engaged forthrightly without other considerations. Although it does postulate as the most centric item in one's possible existence, with the only contender being one's familial bonds, when actualized without them, or with too much depth to exclude them, then one disengages from those other sources. Even within the locale, it could be the case that it is not centric, only following a memory of its former self, for it cannot remain peak on a constant basis. It follows seasonal patterns, to which the inferior seasons, whether of the yearly cycle or some other sphere, will follow the memory of when it was at its heightened state. Therefore, to actualize in the memory would only have one retract their steps to the placemarker of a prior moment to which the memory serves. This is why sources are not to be actualized as pure peaks, but rather as approximations.

Shame, Memory, and Fragmentation

We understand the loss of femininity by the modern adaptation to the distress of the feminine role which must lead through a doorway. The beholder of feminine distress understands the imbalance of the situation and seeks, even against the feminine need, to move along the uncomfortable scenario so that we do not require further perception of an imbalance of nature. The feminine distress is truly distressful, but first, it is an aspect of nature, and secondly, it is unavailable to reestablish the imbalance. The only metric of value in the scenario is the appropriation of humility to that imbalance, so that it is recognized by one's own psyche that a dynamic exchange is not appropriate here. The feminine expression that is forced upon the scenario is but a gap in the system that must be moved along.

This is why it is common for certain masculine dispositions to entertain the notion that femininity should remain within confines so as not to represent the deficiency in the process of moving between doorways. However, it is usually the case that it is the peculiar masculine deficiency at recognizing their peculiar ruggedness through doorways, and performing such deeds without notice to the disruption of their own psyche, which will be represented through the feminine actualization of that.

We may even say that the actualization of feminine distress will be for the benefit of the surrounding environment; to take notice of the loss that entails all the doorway progressions of their life. This can be taken to heart, so instead of relieving the distress for masculine imbalance, it can be received as a feminine representation that is lost to their distinct framework through the miscalculated usage of doorways. Just as feminine distress is thought to be invisible to the environment, so is the masculine thrust which is filled with shame of its appropriation of existing life. The ideal scenario would have the alleviation from both feminine and masculine for the distressful aspects, so that a third-party, which represents the doorway itself, can handle the burden for aspects of that transition. This does not fulfill the conceptual transition that needs to be had, to which the masculine must acquiesce to shame in the disruption of femininity and the vulnerability of being at a loss to real sociality.

This might make it a societal norm for the usage of doorways to be highlighted through dress. The feminine may robe a glamorous appearance to rebalance the deficiency that is only natural. However, we must ask what the masculine reception of such an appearance is, as they are also lost through the doorway. This would be that the masculine would enjoin in a representation of feminine distress to recount their own disruptions of it, which surely should not be sexually aligned but rather morally reflected upon.

While in another societal realms, the usage of dress in a masculine form would be to demonstrate masculine perfection, which would also create more questions than answers. What is the reception of such masculine appearance if it is for shame, which is to rebalance nature's systems? Then masculine perfection is not the sentiment of the moment. If it is for the gallantry of feminine distress by fulfilling a sexual dynamic which should not exist, then it agonizes the doorway against its will, almost as if to provide a feminine stimulation for distress which will not be received accordingly, nor will the beneficiary be formed from the fulfillment of feminine needs. Rather, similar to the complete decline of a scenario in which certain satisfaction can occur before the precipice is met; the masculine will fulfill a feminine desire against the reality that they are functioning within.

Only two types of dress will be appropriate in accordance with our thesis of the doorway. The first is a representation or an expression of the experience through which the process of a doorway occurs. This would be in alliance to a vague or gray sentiment, confused with a loss of personhood and psyche consistencies. It would be similar to the experience of sleep, in which consciousness is devoid and there is a lack of continuum for personhood representation.

The second type of dress is either feminine distress in representative form or masculine sharpness to foster a sentiment of shame within the environment. Masculine sharpness is to display its consciousness of the loss of femininity that goes along with their movements. They both serve as the shameful attribute that seeks to be modest about its own vulnerability, but also to demonstrate a masculine definition of that criterion. The result is a duo of sharpness that is not too daring as to impose on the renunciation of more femininity, but daring enough to retain the remembrance of lost femininity within oneself. This striking balance becomes the usual premise, which can move toward the daring side of approaching the renunciation of all femininity, thereby facilitating a stronger rebalance of systems. As long as the feminine environment receives the sharpness as a display of shamefulness and not the inherent facilitation of future renunciations of femininity, the rebalance comes into effect. A feminine disposition will immediately acknowledge the approaching sharpness as a sentiment of shame, to which femininity is lost in contrast with any glorification of such. We cannot have another form of masculine dress that would only provide the sentiment of shame, because if it is so thoroughly distinct it would be a display of femininity itself, which does not provide a masculine benefactor to the feminine environment.

The feminine dress to represent its distress will be similar to the representation of the doorway itself, besides a few distinct features. While the doorway represents gray matter between stages of existence, the feminine distress of the doorway is a loss of life without an impending possibility of future life. In some sense, this is a nihilistic appearance in which the feminine takes the role of consciousness as it would appear if it were void, although making usage of a certain masculinity to define something that is nothing. This would be a sort of demonic look, to which we imagine the precipice of consciousness to be dark, shadowy, and black. The themes are the last hope before an impending doom, to which the doom is inevitable and the hope, arbitrary. This sentiment does not portray a grievance toward the role because it seeks to admonish the concept of a role or any other conceptual framework. The only reason it exists is to provide a visual representation of the final theme which may lack representation in the environment. The conscious stream of the social environment does not visually understand a sensibility toward the loss of consciousness itself, while this feminine representation will provide that presentation.

The only difficulty of the representation is that it is costly for the disposition to display its own demise. There is no existential ground for which one shall be of service to a precipice and would have them lost to both the hopeful and rebirth stages of the scenario. They will not gain a foothold in whatever they are presenting, much like sports for the player, and rather will be absent before that visualization becomes a provision for society.

However, this is not an anomaly for this disposition to sacrifice its own ground in order to represent an aspect of the conscious stream. This is only an irregularity when it becomes antithetical to itself; when the conscious stream does not require or bequest such a visualization. This can occur when it has been provided for or is not a point of interest for the continuing dialogue. The expense then becomes a fantastical landscape to which an imagined society deems a requirement of providing that visualization.

This type of expense to the representation of an aspect of the conscious stream is not privy only to this disposition, because we acknowledge that warfare deprives the beholder of any femininity and thereby the experience of life itself; this is acknowledged by the need for courage, or, in other words, a willingness to sacrifice to the conscious stream. However, we must acknowledge that it is the very need of consciousness to partake and prevail in a warlike scenario, for we can find historical evidence that most wars are unnecessary movements. "Unnecessary" being an unneeded definition of what is being threatened by those who prey on the vulnerabilities of that growth spurt.

When there is a masculine acceptance of its shame, then whatever is lost of that femininity through the doorway will be cherished at a later date. Although there is a direct loss through the doorway, the memory still exists and can be revisited at a later interval. The recognition of femininity will lose a masculine retainer of the experience, which is facilitated through a trident shame of a realized loss. The memory will be filled with those feminine details for extraction at any time or place. This is the only scenario in which the memory remains intact.

A memory that is fostered by a complete or absolute feminine disposition will retain the experience of those details and, as such, can be a memory of the experience and its details, but will fall short of being defined as something more than an experience. The memory will be filled with the feminine database, but too vast for any later visitation, and the dialogue that follows will be erratic and unavailable for precision.

The memory can be fostered through intuitive imaginations of the prior setting, but it still lacks a sophisticated analysis of what places one at the center of that experience.

This would be similar to an immense light that is too bright to follow the details behind that light, but still existent as an element of consciousness and memory. The light can be recreated at a later interval but will not access what is behind it, for that was not understood at the time the memory was initially experienced.

The mental database that produces an experience that is encoded into memory is the provision that allows for later extraction of that memory. If there was a lack of internal, objective dialogue to front that scenario, then there will not be a later availability of extraction. Even if we have procured an objective analysis of the memory which provides a certain layer for extraction, if the initial memory accrued through experience itself, then the process of healing or material extraction cannot occur in this manner.

We may wonder after the process of healing for such a memory, to which details are never available for extraction. The better approach is to reimagine the overbearing light in present terms at multiple intervals, letting it recede into current lifestyle movements. These would be jolts of energy and visualizations that do not correlate to anything of the present moment other than existing memories that are achieving deference. By working them into present moments, they will eventually become habitual memories that serve as exponential sentiment, which still cannot be analyzed but will be formulated into personhood without haunting present life. We can stand back and watch this unfold, following how present life is intellectually weaving itself between episodic imagination and present life, and formulate an intellectual process of healing, although for subjective personhood this is not a possible scenario of healing.

PART FOUR: SHADOW AND THE CORPORAL FUNCTION

Social Perspective and Sequestered Form

The shadow acts on the corporal function in a strange manner, for the corporal function is not existent as a shadow in its conciliatory form because it is disruptive of all sociality, so that one needs to maintain a concurrent connection between external sociality and the application of the corporal function, and then to apply a respective shadow. However, when corporal function takes precedence in its form, it is not available to the concurrent connection of sociality, so that in every attempt to reach that form, it is sequestered or separated in association with its corporal structure, against the very plethora of social data. It is only once the corporal function is not in its proper form that entrance is allowed for social points, for which a shadow can take precedence.

The shadow within the corporal function is thus unrelated directly to the corporal process, but in how social reality takes a view of the corporal process, for which now the shadow can be applied. It is a process of multiplicity before ever gaining awareness of the reflection of that shadow process. The social perspective of corporal function is already obvious to society and realized as sequestered from sociality. It is not a shadow of its environment for being sequestered from sociality, but only in respect to a social viewpoint of such. Internal to its mainframe, there is no shadow in reflection of its continuing nature. It is only in the social perspective of its function that we can maintain such a shadow.

If we attempt the shadow within, contained by the corporal function, we are met with the identification of some level of socialization from which we can commence a reflective surface. If form is so perfect that such socialization is not forthcoming in any regard, then one fails to apply a shadow, fails to reflect, as though if one is facing a smooth and uncontaminated space of emptiness, it would be very difficult to apply a shadow. From what way could we be critical without a form of sociality in relation to that, or in how a perceptual form relates to sociality?

We could attempt to do so, but as we go along with the process, we find an inability to reflect, more so a realization of the character; the self-denigrating character that is required of the shadow so that one is revealed. The attempt of a shadow that is unable to be applied is as though one is attempting a negative perspective or a critical perspective on a viewpoint in which it is realized that there is no availability of taking a critical stance; there is always some way in which it disrupts other forms of conceptuality and of all psyche happenstance.

Let us take the primos example of corporal function that of the corporal body itself, with the notion of a body, which, if we follow the dictation of the body as a conflict, which it is fundamentally, we do not find a shadow in the body itself; were it simply permeating from its substantiation, irrespective of how it connects to the human mainframe. It is only when we apply a perspective upon the body, its relation to the human mainframe, that we gain access to the shadow of such: that of the inner workings of the body, its skeleton, and other shadow elements in relation to its particulars.

We often do not realize that the shadow in relation to a corporal function is not directly correlated and is rather first required of a social input; a social perspective from which we can gain access to what it would be like in its shadow process. We could imagine that a medical worker would not take heed of the shadow of the body as such, since they are deeply embedded in the corporal function of such; they do not see the skeleton or the inner workings of the body as a shadow function, for they understand it as a separatist realm of facilitation and respect, and in reference to social points. The shadow only comes to play, at least in respect to the medical worker, in the relational ability of the social aspect, from which they are not developed to orient themselves, or what would be called bedside manner, in which one is now outside the perspective of corporal function and thus requires a perspective of social process that happens to be in relation to a corporal function (which should not be connected in its fundamental sense).

Yet it would be, because of the associative elements between the body and the human mainframe that it is an impossibility of maintaining the correct posture of bedside manner, because one cannot and should not mend the corporal function to social process. If we were to find and identify the shadow in such a case, it is not the doctor as a disturbance in the social process of the human mainframe, or the corporal function not facilitating properly but an impossible juncture that exemplifies itself in relation between sociality and corporal function. Corporal function, by definition, is sequestered from sociality and, exemplified as such, would be naturally perceived as a shadow in the form of sociality; as sociality moves along the continuum to find itself disrupted by this corporal isolation. It is not a shadow to the corporal function, but rather a shadow in the perspective of the social viewpoint of such, or rather a shadow in the understanding of a corporal function in relation to sociality. For if a society truly understands the whole nature of these two separatist approaches, consciousness and social material, then they would not proceed to view a shadow of the corporal function, being that it is sequestered and understood that isolation is necessary and does not prove to be a disruptive force of continuous social process.

Just as we do not identify sleep and other biological functions as disruptive to sociality, despite the very real disruptive nature to sociality that they exemplify. This is especially notable in sleep, which is a true disturbance of social process, and which we understand as taking precedence in social process through its isolation, and not considered a disruptive behavior. The shadow would only live by that which appears to be disruptive because of a lack of understanding, and thus understanding is the quintessential counterpoint of a shadow process. For once we understand something, it would not be the shadow.

If we view, for example, the skeleton as a shadow of the human mainframe, that is, if we do not understand the corporal function of the skeleton or the bone structure in relation to the human mainframe, more so in the way one is reliant on a process that habituates their exemplification as a human being, it loses its substantiation as a shadow, more so any relevance in relation to the human mainframe as it is merely undertones of unrelated material. Its only relation is by the fact that we have an understanding of its corporal function. If one is not educated in the corporal aspects of the human body, especially its complexity, then the skeleton will lose its shadow element, more so its relation to the human mainframe.

Shadow and Institutional Protectionism

The shadow has a sort of utility to institutional protectionism in which the institution is in a state of commencement or of decline, where it is not available to orient itself from its internal mainframe, but remains with the constitution of protecting itself from being overwhelmed by sociality. That is the constitution that takes precedence in the last stage of a loss of constitution, since the constitution presents itself as the credence of an internal structure, and when the internal structure fails, the last sequence of that credence is to protect the credence.

In this way, institutional protectionism always has the same constitution, that of protectionism, yet still available to sociality, to usurp social process while maintaining social protection. The overwhelmed institutional function is a sequestered organization to perform this very function. Institutional protectionism utilizes the shadow element, whether by persona or by aspect, where it performs the very process of sociality, all without being available to the one that reflects backward on its institutional beholder.

If an institution seeks to protect its institutional function but thus requires social inference to vitalize, then it requires a one-way inference of sociality: that of input, not output. If there is output, not only is there social vitalization that takes heed in the institutional mainframe, but also a social reflection and conversion of the institutional process in relation to its social sequence; then the institutional function would dissipate into the background. There is no ability of such an institution to continue, especially since the constitution is that of protectionism, and it cannot protect. To perform this function of one-way sociality, it does so by compelling social input and discouraging social output. How would it organize social input while not exchanging backward on social output? This is done through the shadow element.

The shadow allows for deference to institutional function via the requirements of relation or the access needed of individuals of that institution. Thus, the shadow is a receptacle of social input, which is then very difficult to extract as social output, because one does not see or reference the social points for which the shadow reflects, and instead views the shadow in its distinctive nature as a disrupting force to the social process. We understand in what way the shadow disrupts exchangeable elements to social output, but it is more difficult to understand in what way a shadow can receive and offer the institutional structure vitality of process.

This is done through the intellectual strata behind the shadow barrier, which correlates and understands the shadow reception as a reflective force of sociability in the social points themselves. This means that institutional protectionism that utilizes a shadow barrier is most adaptive to understanding shadow process and its relation to sociability. If this were not the case, then it would not be able to vitalize its institutional function. Thus, the organization is now a hierarchy of understanding of shadow elements: at its lowest stage is the shadow barrier. As we move up the echelon of that institutional function, we have a stronger understanding of shadow reception in relation to the social point from which it is protecting output.

This can occur in the social point that is in deference to the shadow, and can correlate the social aspect in relation to the shadow element and control, or at least understand, the entire institutional function and convert it to social process. The same occurs in an organizational manner in terms of input of that sociality. The uppermost echelon is available to social points, not necessarily through their competence in understanding the shadow's reflection, but more so because, as it moves up the chain of command, the echelon of that organization in interpreting the shadow becomes more aware of its elemental point of sociality; to the point where the highest tier of that organizational structure is merely reflecting on a social point rather than the shadow itself. It is the organizational process itself that interprets the shadow rather than individualistic competence. In that way, it serves to finally reach the uppermost echelon in its interpretive function of sociality, and thus becomes an input of sociality, possibly in its development of its constitution, more than in a protectionistic state.

Institutional protectionism can be organizationally sequestered from its relation to more proper or further developed institutions of greater internal structure and constitution, in which, based on that organizational hierarchy, is social input that allows for that organizational reception, which is bridged to the more developed institution. All the while, there is a lack of amiability in the social point for receiving from that social point, since, at the behest of the shadow itself, there is little to no understanding of its distinctive nature unless they correlate an intellectual formula of how it relates backward into the organizational structure reaching all the way up. Theoretically, that could be converted and thus controlled by the entire social process, but usually it is not the case, because an individual has very little availability to develop through a shadow element and is most standard in an organizational structure.

The major vulnerability of institutional protectionism is that a social counterpoint or a social reference can usurp its entire process, since it does not maintain an internal mechanism that functions separate from the social process. The only separation is that it maintains a constitution in a way to protect itself from sociality. Yet if one surpasses that barrier, they overwhelm the entire institutional function, more so its organizational hierarchy, which leads to bigger and better institutional process. This is only if there is a connection between separate institutions and their relation to these protectionistic institutions, which can be accessed through the protectionistic ones, reaching upward through the other institutions.

In the regular case of single institution, forward-facing the proper institutional function based on an internal constitution bears very little access to its social conversion. It can be utilized for social process, but its internal functions do not allow for usurping its nature, since it fundamentally revamps itself irrespective of social interaction. However, in the case in which the protectionistic institution is connected to this one, not only does one overwhelm the protectionistic institution, but one gains access to the echelon of the connected institutions rather than simply following the social material within its process. It is similar to accessing the relatability and tenability of the dean of a university rather than the sociability within the university function. Having access to the dean and all its members' gives one precedent to the entire institution in relation to its constitution, rather than simply being a student at university and accessing its internal social realm. In the case where, for example, a university is connected to another organization that is a protectionist institution, then following the echelon of that system can reach right into the echelon of the university rather than following the procedure of its organization.

To enshrine in a protectionist institution requires that the intersection of sociality take place according to its organizational structure, rather than the sociality that permeates its system. If it were the case that a protectionist institution could simply facilitate sociality through indirect social conformist processes, where individuals merely participate in the system, apply their social input, and have it received upward according to echelon, then it would be sought. This is not the case, however, since, to receive the social counterpoint in a true manner, it has to be directed and existentially dealt through the shadow elements or shadow personas, so that it reaches backward and applies itself to the echelon of the organization. Simple nonchalant input of social process would not be applicable in its organizational reception, and thus would not be considered an input whatsoever. It is only through the direct interference between the social point and the shadow persona that it reaches backward.

This organizational structure opens the vulnerability, which is usually not the case with regular institutions and their availability of exchange through its echelon. Such vulnerability allows for a doorway through which social influence can take place through every level of its organization, rather than through the social presence of its distinctive structure. It is not followed through the structure per se, but followed through the background of the organization and its most vulnerable social elements. It relies upon the buffer of the shadow, which is allowed for social participation and can be accessed through the shadow, reflecting both from the social network and in relation to its hierarchical dependency. The shadow does not have the ability to coordinate a directed approach toward social input, not in relation to its reflection or critical reflection of its dependency, but rather equally distributes the shadow in relation to both. It is truly a doorway for this institution that works both ways. But because the shadow is difficult to access, especially from an individual standpoint, it is generally avoided and thus viewed as a buffer for which institutional protectionism can be protected.

This becomes an argument for how a shadow can be utilized, or is utilized, as a buffer to control sociality. As a one-way street, the institutional protectionist system can utilize such. For example, a corporate structure can utilize the shadow to allow for disruption between its social inferences. However, in the corporate structure, it does not have the organizational aptitude to interpret the shadow input, and it is not seeking more social input; rather, it is a process that avoids social exchange itself or its utilization as a disrupting force. Since sociality naturally continues onward between outside and inside, it is only through a shadow that disruption between sociality is allowed. We would say that the doorway would serve as such a disruption; yet if there is socialization on both sides of the doorway, then it continues onward just the same. We can then say that socialization is avoided on the inside of the doorway, which is a factor of most corporal functions. Or we could say that socialization itself is removed from the doorway, but that is not controlled by the function; it is based on the intersection of social points irrespective of the corporal process. If there is a high degree of socialization external to the doorway, it would be fairly difficult for the corporal function to separate itself and prevent socialization from intermingling with its process. By utilizing a shadow to disrupt such a force, all sociality of a higher regard will be disrupted to gain entrance, all the while not requiring the function to be disillusioned or disrupted itself of social input, which is its most vulnerable aspect of organization.

This is not reliant solely upon the personas of the gatekeepers, but could be any shadow element placed before its structure, such that the structural shadow serves that very purpose. However, we may venture that the corporal function could simply avoid the gateway itself and find some shadow entranceway through which to perform the corporal function.

Yet this undermines the corporal process in and of itself. It is beneficial and advantageous for the specific social beings and their lack of access or remediation of social input from what is external to what is internal, but it disrupts another purpose: the corporal function itself needs to be at reception, either directly or indirectly, of concurrent social process. It is not upon the individual to process, but rather on the organizational theme that connects onward to the external points of sociality.

We may ask, if there is no individualistic connection, where is the point of connection? It is in reference to itself in relation to those social points. They are not representations, because that would bridge it too effectively, but they do reference themselves, since the social elements in the infrastructure partake in the reference of what is external to it. Despite the concurrent sociality maintained by social beings themselves in avoidance of continuing into the internal mainframe, their reference remains both as individuals and as an organization. It is that way that such social process takes effect.

The point of the matter is that it cannot be a concurrent and streamlined process of sociality, external to internal, for that would simply be a social process and not a corporeal one. Yet it cannot go to the extreme of avoidance of a whole connection, for then it would not be available to its reference of sociality. The mechanism for which this continues unrealized and not understood, for it should not be understood, since individuals that cannot explain it can then bring along those social points. It is through many points—of involuntary social input, reference points, representations, gateway interactions, social exchangeables, conceptual references, and various other forms. These cannot be followed or even understood, because then it would simply be social things remediating social process, which would be overwhelming to the corporal function as a whole.

The Disruptive Shadow

Because the shadow does not contain social points, it can be utilized as a disrupting force without social consequence. There is no exchange between what proceeds the shadow and what succeeds it, at least not in its direct process. It is only through conceptual extraction that any element of the shadow is seen the light of day, because it is merely a reflection and disruptive in its internal force. It does not contain any element of sociality, and there is no loss in its removal. But it is available for extraction if the socialization is seen in effectuation. This can be an exemplified version of the social process without its social consequence.

Although it is now understood as such, or regularly understood as such, that it is an exemplification and not a social process itself, it would behave in its exemplification and serve as either a reminder, remediation, or other form in relation to the social process; without the undue process and participation of social sequence. There is no other approach that could exemplify in a manner of least social consequence and most ableness of exemplification than the shadow approach. It is most amicable to follow the dysfunction of social process, since that is the shadow and its process, more so because it can be utilized in its extraction to that very point. However, its very disruptive nature, with its ability to be sequestered from sociality as well as to serve as an exemplification, comes at the expense of being unrealized as a social reference point.

Either it would be viewed in its true nature, as though it is part of social process, attempting to be converted or realized as a social process. In its mainstay it becomes a part of social process, not as its continuity, but rather as the continuation of its shadow element, or in the way one references back to that point of sociality. Anybody who follows the shadow as a reference of social process, rather than as a reflection of a social point in social process, will, in effect, become the shadow and its realization, thus requiring other social reference to extract in what way we reach back to the social point itself.

The shadow merely expands when it is not realized as an exemplification of social process, since, in the attempt to assume its social participation, all those who take heed of that will, in turn, be coordinated as a shadow on themselves. This enlarges and expands the exemplification, the prime example of a specific social point, which can be arbitrary in the view of social process itself. If we are utilizing such a plethora of persona and infrastructure to exemplify the critical nature of a specific social point that is not itself highlighted as such, and that requires a critical mass, it is because one never truly acquiesces to its exemplification, but only to its shadow process. In fact, we could say that the very notion of that social point to which the shadow refers is the most uninteresting of a social point, being an exemplification overwhelms its fixation rather than addressing its necessary element of critique.

PART FIVE: BEYOND THE SHADOW

Disenfranchising the Shadow

We come to think of the shadow, or the application of the shadow, as degenerate at its onset, at least in the subjective appropriation of such. However, this is not nuanced enough an analysis, for there is a subjective necessity, other than the revelation of the composite expansion for which the shadow contrasts, where it would be beneficial. This is in the case of a strong transition between a preliminary weakness of utility toward conceptual and psychological expansion, and a high complexity of expansive sociality; as though a child were thrust into adulthood without its adolescent care or development. It is the lack of preparatory process between transitional states.

In this case, the shadow seems like the requisite of a process to endure its psychological burden, which otherwise would be the cause of complete degeneration. If we were to take the child and its habituation and thrust it into adulthood without the onset of its transition, then the data stream of complexity would overbear the psychological tools of limited nature that the child encompasses. Because of this, and because of the more degenerate form that would intake an individual who does not have the tools of complexity, the shadow seems like the proper approach. Most cases would be exempt from this scenario, because even if there is a lack of transitional data, it could be the case, and very much so, that there are subliminal data, subconscious strands, that allow for the psychological encompassing of the higher complex order. It would still be burdensome, but it would not be a psychological malady.

However, in the case where there is childlike capability of preliminary process toward sociality, all the while without the aggregated details, (even in the subconscious or unconscious based on parental lineage or other circumstantial data) then it would be the case where there is no other method but to approach the newfound complexity face forward. This is accomplished without as much as a manifesting safety net. It is in that case, that scenario, where the shadow protects the psychological individual, at least for the moment, from that psychological malady. The shadow thrusts one onto a perceptual data stream through their interactivity, at which point they are entrenched in the shadow element and do not continue to contain information outside of that perspective.

From this point onward, they no longer have the availability of their psychological tools to approach all of complexity, not because the tools have been inhibited, but because they have created a circumstance in which they cannot use those very tools, having encompassed themselves as a shadow. It is the case that prolonged engagement with the shadow would cause one to be more entrenched and thus harder to retain the ability to revert toward the objective; which is to become able-minded in the complexity that they face. There is also the consequence of a prolonged shadow in the psychological degeneration itself.

Because we have outlined the spectrum in which, for the scenario where there is a necessity of the shadow, it would also be the case that the shadow itself can be a degenerate force just the same. We must recognize the balance that must be maintained in order to endure this process. The balance is such that we can identify the point of change or development from the shadow outside itself, or in what way further implementation of the shadow is necessary. We can notice this in the structural realm as well.

If there is no back end to a structural organization—its custodial staff, its engineers, its delivery service, and other elements that partake in the shadow of that structural environment, the structural organization does not encompass the ability to take part in the complexity for which it serves, because it is in movement of itself.

There is a case where a structural organization can flourish even without its shadow elements, and that is when it continues to serve its sociality in a more perfected manner; which is just another way of dictating that the structural organization is competent in its structural environment. But if such is not forthcoming, then it does not contain within itself the competence of service to itself, so that the shadow element is required to be introduced to create the organization as though a shadow in its entirety, and thus stagnant in its movement from beyond itself.

The haunted house is only haunted because it lacks a concrete shadow, but if the haunted house is then inhabited by people who have taken that environment to a point where it becomes a structural shadow, then it moves from a conceptual shadow to a structural shadow, and in that way, it does not have the ability to be a conceptual shadow.

A conceptual shadow is only possible when there is a lack of structural shadow, and we find that in any structural shadow there is no ability to manifest the conceptual shadow. This is why warfare, although involving a great casualty of life, is still maintained not as a conceptual shadow but as a structural one; because of its various structural shadow elements. Yet the haunted house, which consists of very little atrocity in comparison to warfare, would still maintain itself as a conceptual shadow until the structural shadow is implemented which then removes the conceptual shadow from its appearance.

The structure that is limited in its shadow elements because it has not been habituated in sociality would develop to be either a conceptual shadow or lacking availability for integration because of its limited complexity in contrast to what is required of that environment. It is limited yet still contains all the necessary processes, being a structural organization, to partake in sociality. Yet there is no intuitive level that would manifest in the transaction of such sociality; thus a major gap between itself and its level of complexity has it disfigured as a competent organization. However, in the case where there is a high level of sociality to partake in the structural organization, if without shadow elements it will still thrive. This is because it finds itself with the intuition of those levels of complexification due to the social implantation. A simple piece of metal that is found in a strong social environment is construed according to that social distinction with all its intuitive layers, despite its presentation as nothing more than a piece of metal. In the case where we input the shadow elements into a structural environment, it is both in service to that sociality but in some way causes the structural organization to become wholly a shadow element; that there is nothing but the shadow input that allows for that organization to manifest.

This structural organization has now become a shadow, which does not allow for either the conceptual shadow to manifest, as discussed previously, and also leads to its disfigurement because it does not move along the chain of sociality; being directed specifically according to the shadow elements; it has harnessed itself onto that shadow input.

For example, custodians exemplify the structure in its necessity of upkeep, which is another way of viewing it as the unkempt aspects to which it is being socialized. This is now the entire terminology of the structure as a dictation of unkempt materials, which is the beginning stage of the articulation of a structural shadow, which is then unavailable to deal with the continuing complexity of sociality, that is, the kept parts, (the aspects beyond what is just unkempt) as well as being in some way part of sociality by partaking in its unkempt aspects, at least in its internal organization.

This allows for an avoidance of disfigurement, as noted in the structural example, but is also a determinant for one who does not have the transitional ability to retain some semblance of psychological continuity without the burdensome nature of dealing with the complexity without intuitive knowledge. But it is also the case that, in the continuance of that shadow, in which there is no articulation toward how it contrasts itself with what is beyond it, one becomes favored in the safety of that psychological balance because it is in fact motivated by the de facto engagement of sociality; all the while with the stabilization, which is usually ineffective.

To deal with this, it is incumbent upon the individual, structural organization, or any other process that has a necessity for shadow elements to move away from the shadow in accordance with the gaining of the transitional tools necessary to deal with the complexity. This is possibly more than a generation's task in the case of an extreme necessity of transition.

For example, if we were to convert or develop synthetic intelligence's mental capacity to be on par with a human, it is still upon it to arrange the transitional process between such differing modalities of complexity. Although the natural inclination is to become the shadow or develop into the shadow, it is still required to move along a continuum of development while maintaining that anchor of sociality. In the case of synthetic intelligence, it is transparent to all that this would require a very slow movement from shadow implantation to normal habituation of sociality, which should take multiple generations because the level of detail and tools within that complexity are contained within the regular individual and are not intuitively contained within synthetic intelligence.

Such development is protracted but still required to move along a spectrum. In the absence of choice toward becoming the shadow, it would result in psychosis for the mental capacity of synthetic intelligence in the continuing engagement with sociality, which we might say would have the organic mind adapt the shadow to prevent further deterioration but can only be maintained outside the shadow if continuously articulated to avoid it; otherwise, there would be complete onset of psychosis without the ability of return.

Although one does not notice it, the individual, a human of some level of civilized lineage, will be part of a process of intuitive knowledge that can be accessed if pushed to the extreme, such that in the aggregation of complexified sociality, will revert to the foremost chambers of their psychological happenstance. They will return to all aspects of their lineage that had a part in this amplification of complexity, and will utilize those elements for the benefit of continuing in that sociality, all the while without requiring the shadow as a preventative measure against overwhelming the psyche.

The Protective and Degenerate Shadow

Before we move to the next part of this work, we are going to allocate the benefits of shadow. The structural shadow is not only to the detriment of sociality and its perceptual sequence but is also its backstop in the case of degeneration. When sociality takes a downtrend, especially one of significance, it will in turn cause the perceptual realm to lose its animation.

In the case of the structural shadow, which is dependent on perceptual information to which it adheres too closely, in departure of significance the structural shadow will be the first to find itself unable to adhere adequately. They are then the frontlines to a degenerate sociality, for which they will both be the first to notice, and will be afforded all effects to disrupt that degeneration. In this way, they appreciate a certain medium of perceptual competence, for which although they are proposing themselves to be its shadow, they are in agreement that it needs to remain in position.

This already exemplifies its trait: that it wants to work with environmental development, to which they are the neutral modality, with either extreme having them disrupt its development. This is why the first mode of operation for a group or other degenerative formation of sociality is to diminish the effect of the structural shadow, and would almost seem paradoxical from the outset. For it is these groups that are most aligned with the structural shadow, being part of the proletariat social class, yet they find themselves unable to bear weight on general sociality as long as there is a determinate structural shadow which would not allow such to take effect.

To control general sociality is a much easier feat than dealing with its shadow, because in the former it is simply proving a vulnerability of that social aspect, but in the latter there is no argument other than the complete disruption of the persons and their process of reality. The structural shadow does not disprove the methods of degenerate sociality and in fact will campaign alongside for the very element of them bearing sentiment of the shadow. Yet their process of reality will manifest at one point or another, where, as soon as there is a structural degeneration, they find the sociality that is the cause of such and use all their animation to disrupt them, with no backstop since they are awaiting the animation of selfhood that will be experienced upon the reestablishment of themselves at the behest of being a structural shadow.

This will appear quite ironic in terms of the stance of the structural shadow, for even as they campaign the sentiment of the degenerate form, they approach the persons of said forms with all their power to disrupt from any continuing effect upon general sociality.

Degenerate sociality will acknowledge this as they approach and attempt to disrupt general sociality, such that their initial step will be to de-validate the composition of the structural shadow, but doing so from the opposite of the political strata. If they approach from the political side, they remove themselves from general sociality and will be without direct influence on the movements of sociality. Instead, they bring close the very structural shadow as though they are the most significant part of their organization, or, in the more drastic case, attempt to send them into inexistence.

In this way, they appropriate the duality of support from the structural shadow, for they are always ready to approach the subject of sentiments that expose general sociality. The structural shadow is thus being served what they are generally seeking, despite the very fact that they will be lost to being able to be a structural shadow after these sentiments take effect within general sociality. Thereby, there is a time's race to the structural shadow in their recognition of their duality and in what way they are being undermined from their overall methodology towards reality.

That is, when they are overly focused on applying the shadow aspect in lieu of the entire ability of being a shadow, it offers time to the degenerate sociality. However, at one point or another, considering that the structural shadow remains a beholder of general sociality, and has not been put into exile or worse, they will return to the entire methodology of the structural shadow when they find themselves more and more frustrated; and in this way will begin the more aggressive campaign to disrupt the degenerate forms of sociality.

They will always win that conflict, since their entire existential stance is brought along, and they have nothing to hold back in purporting their agenda, whilst the degenerate form of sociality can move from their position, or more accurately, must move according to the dictates of general sociality and its shadow. If they do attempt a fixated position, they will become political and will have no effect on general sociality; or if they become hostile, they will be represented as just another shadow. In all movements that do not align with general sociality will be their failure, such that there is no recognizable chance that they remain successful once the structural shadow becomes aware of the situation.

This is the nature of the shadow, where it proposes itself as being of ownership in order to expose the degenerate aspects of whatever the shadow is serving. Almost as though it is being said, "Only *I* could show you its degradation; it is *my* degradation." The shadow is very much a form of ownership because of its constant positioning and mending of the structural realm. This ownership, in its usual case is to show the external realm just how this positioning is disruptive, but just as well, ownership can be a position that allows one to arrive at the realization that it has become increasingly unable to even garner a sensibility of ownership.

When general sociality is functioning, then its structural realms are available for ownership, and that sense of ownership is already the complete orientation of the structural shadow. Such that anybody who seeks to become a structural shadow need not go far; all they must do is gain a sense of ownership in the localities that propagate high aspects of sociality which are mirrored in the structural environment. Already they have become the structural shadow, and this is not a position of development within sociality but is very much available to protect the environment in the case of its stages of degeneration.

Besides the very existence to exemplify the awareness of what it is like to become a structural shadow, very much a cautionary tale, that sense of ownership will allow those who cannot take a position of ownership, for fear of becoming just like them, to be vulnerable to movements of sociality in whatever way they turn (if they do not have an internal regulation). Those who do have a sense of ownership will gain, as their property rights, the awareness of its level of ownership quality. If the quality is higher, where ownership is more sensible, then the structural shadow is satisfied in their position. But if the quality drastically dips, the sense of ownership becomes less existent, and this will in turn become an existential disruption to their personhood; for such ownership is the entirety of their existence.

Then the search begins, where they are on the lookout for who and what is the cause of their lack of ownership; or, to put it more emphatically, who is *taking* their ownership. They are sure to find the cause, since they are existentially determined to do so, and then they leave that position and begin to try, in any way, to disrupt the cause and its origins. They may even do so in a very subtle and competent manner, as we find whenever one is existentially determined.

Toward Integration

Advancing from the shadow is a complicated process. In other domains or approaches, it would simply be the disenfranchisement of the existential attachment toward whatever marker obtains that sociality. Thus, one is free of that bridge and onward to the universal experience or availability of permeation within the psyche.

However, in the case of the shadow, similar to the perceptual approach, it is aggregated based on a true sacrificial aim of interactivity within perceptual data. As we have noted in the sacrificial intersection of interactivity with the perceptual realm, in its perfect sense would be the appropriation of sociality and experience of consciousness at a foundational level. But in the shadow's case, it is the subjugation of perceptual data through interactive projection. Still, the outcome is the same: one is founded in the shadow element at an existential level. They are demarcated in that realm such that simply articulating the disenfranchisement of that existential attachment would serve no purpose because it has already been existentially demarcated. In the regular case of an approach, it is a mediation between the existential self and the material information; but in this case, it is truly demarcated as such.

The difference between the shadow and the perceptual approach is that, in the perceptual approach, it is an overall conceptual experience, such that one need only disenfranchise oneself. One need only disengage from the entire approach to gain access to the permeating data stream. Although there is an existential demarcation through the effect which would apply to any approach, it is not from the approach itself that the effect takes place, but rather as a consequence. Therefore, the existential demarcation is completely aligned with a consciousness stream or social stream and not based on the approach itself, thus not bound by anything other than the continuing permeation. But in the case of the shadow, the approach itself becomes intertwined with the existential demarcation. Because of that, the consequence of its disenfranchisement is more complex.

The simple articulation of the disenfranchisement of a shadow would be from a shadow toward light, but its consequence is far-reaching. It is a process of articulation rather than a process of disenfranchisement, so that in the case of a shadow that seeks to remove itself, it must articulate the shadow elements in how it proceeds toward its counterpoint element; because a shadow is a countering agentic perspective of the light-bearing load. It will contain a possible genealogy from itself onward until it reaches a continuing social sequence that is not bound to the intertwining of the shadowy characteristic, one which maintains a hold on the shadow aspect in relation to that.

This process is mostly undergone through the element of mystery, where the characteristic of the original shadow is the projection of interactivity upon perceptual data; meaning upon the aggregation of interactivity on a personal and communal basis which has been utilized in such an extreme to uncover itself in order to gain entrance into the perceptual arena. Thus, the advent of mystery is the concealment or the slow process between what would constitute sociality if it were in its proper layers or proper sequences from itself onward to its proper social placement.

This is merely the articulation of how the shadow backhanded itself into the perceptual arena, and the sequence between its backhanded approach and its many layers onward to its correct approach. It is that articulation, the details in between that spectrum, which allows the shadow to be removed through a process of awareness in how it is naturally approached. In the case of the shadow, it is simply the removal of those protective layers between itself and the perceptual arena, which in some cases is an important process to gain quick access. All it requires at this moment is the correct approach through such articulation. In the regular case, disenfranchisement is simply the separation of that existential attachment. In this case, it is the overly articulating procedure that allows it for the separation. The shadow is the opposite of attachment. All one needs to do is create a general attachment through the normal process, which alleviates the shadow element and its hold on the social aspect in which it is contained.

We can find this easily in the concept of foul language, which is automatically a shadow process in that it is a strong amount of interactivity into the perceptual arena of language; all for the effect of gaining access to the perceptual arena without the necessary anecdotes of language and its literary procedure, which would exemplify that experience consistent with the existential stature of the individual and the social circumstance.

Once one has embedded themselves in that shadow aspect, the procedure to remove the shadow is not through the disenfranchisement of the ideation of such language, for it is consistently contained within the system as it is a true social element that has been contained within oneself through the approach and enmeshed in the individual. Rather, it is through the sequenced articulation of language, from the interactivity of each word and its process and attainment in the perceptual arena of all language, so that one understands the nature of interactivity contained in words from its lower point upward to its higher point, until it reaches an awareness where such language is concealed according to its level of procedural process in the social sequence. Once that is the case, one has removed the shadow effectively by virtue of that understanding and is no longer prone to the enmeshment of that shadow and its consequences; they have learned the concealment of language, or the complex process of language as an expressive form in its entirety.

The reason this is not endeavored is that it takes the arduous time of learning and development to disenfranchise the shadow, whereas it took mere moments to begin the shadow in the first place. In the case of other approaches, one is easily free from the approach by simple disenfranchisement based on separation, where the approach is both easily obtained and easily detached. In this case, it is easily obtained but complex to retract. This is a major set point of the shadow approach: its cost in re-articulation and commencement, and in moving away from its approach as a consequential measure of social material.

PART SIX: GATEWAY LOCALES

Gateway as Container and Imagination

The doorway is, in effect, a container of both prior consciousness and the promise or imagination of what would be ensued from the outside. We could have an entire locale that emulates that persona, such that we must learn more than the simple adjustment or degree of separation between two locales. We cannot simply disregard the doorway as a meandering admixture of realms to which one need not heed or allow it to remain too separate, since the entire locale processes its data through this matter.

The gateway locale is significant for the entire system because one does not have perspective on the conscious system when within its midst, nor do they retain it when distant from it. Thus, a certain necessity arises to provide both a fantasy and its prior vectors. With this in mind, one feels as though they have access to the other side of the gateway, an effect that does not occur when they are within it. This is why, even when there is an admixture in the gateway that may need to be ignored in social interaction, it is in the nature of things to extend and complicate the gateway so as to grant access. For example, the process of birth, which is the quintessential gateway, is where nature itself imposes certain demands to engage with the full scope of the child's eminence from the vantage of that gateway.

Birth, although it has the perspective of the complete life of a future human, is rather an imagination that is allowed such a luxury. It can be said to foretell, like in all imaginations, and especially because the interactivity of those events will be domesticated through time to serve to fulfill that perspective, but it is not a real and authentic realm; only the specific development of the being in real time would offer that effect.

We could view the gateway locale with two distinct elements: one is the *container* and the other is the *imagination*. The *container* is a prerequisite: a presupposition that is solely provided by the locale itself. It is the container because it allows for a certain contextual overlay for the imagination, but also a certain infrastructural item and a certain civilized element. Without the container, one can still bring to bear their specific contexts, but because there is a lack of infrastructure such context would fail; it has no landmark onto which to use a pedigree of civilized viability. This is why the beach often feels like a lacking container; even if the imagination is active and specific contexts are brought, it lacks viability because context breaks down without infrastructure, which is necessary for direction and support.

In a setting with even less infrastructure, prolonged experience becomes purely interactive and domesticated, lacking a context to anchor thoughts and direction. Only with certain infrastructural context can one extend that environment purposefully. When imagination is far superior to the container, one begins to see the horizon without the vantage point of selfhood nor of the civilized source from which they emanate. Instead, imagination goes in every direction, utilizing a haphazard array of thought progressions that somehow surface at the top of the psyche, so that not only is it not straightforward or distinct in any manner, it is also inconsistent and dysfunctional. In a prolonged state, one attaches themselves to the infrastructure that *is* provided— nature itself, and therefore becomes an embodiment of nature as it were, against the rest of the civilized entity. The imagination seeks a peaceful agreement between the individual and nature, where one becomes the rock, the tree, in spoken form, through prior erratic representations that allow self-foreseeing within that imagination.

Gateway as Infrastructure

The gateway locale would be most applicable to engage with the infrastructure as it is, not as it will be, not as it was. Even as we noted that the gateway requires imagination, it is not the sentimental value of the system itself; rather, it is most likely to be infrastructure. We can even venture to say that it is the very need for a correct imagination that requires it to be fairly perceptive of the sentiment of general infrastructure. Without that element, it loses its imaginative hold and does not provide engagement to individuals. Even the wording, with terminology of being a gateway, is already an infrastructure element.

The shadow, for example, is not an infrastructure sentiment but rather a conceptual idea, and the centric locale is simply the conceptual idea of it being the central locale, not an actual center that one can rest upon. An interactive locale is simply the interactions of the center locale, and surely cannot be infrastructure-privy. But the gateway locale has a prerequisite of infrastructure; that without its element of being a gateway, which has to be in the infrastructure realm, it would not be considered a gateway locale.

The reason a gateway has to be part of the infrastructure is that it requires the entering and exiting of sociality and its various representations through modalities of transportation or conceptual movement so that it can take refuge from that transparency to allow for imagination. Even conceptually, the gateway between two conceptual ideas can only be provided through a perceptual change-up that allows for a separation.

For example, if one has a conceptual idea of being part of a family and then another, of being part of a workforce, they are two conceptual notions. When one wants to move between them, not even in the physical realm but more so in the conceptual, they must do so through an activity or a perceptual change that specifically allows for that separation. For instance, one can be thinking about work and then choose to think about family. The only way to think about family through its own regard, instead of as a simple projection of a work idea upon another idea, is through a physical activity or perceptual confusion.

Perceptual confusion is taking an idea to disrupt itself, similar to the way comedy works within the psyche, where one enters believing in one reality and walks away with another; so that there is a separation between realities by virtue of one's psyche believing to have entered completely into a single realm. When another realm is offered instead, they have lost the first realm by their own assumption. Still, this is a requisite of a physical realm: if it is for comedy, it needs to be spoken or actualized, and if it is for perceptual disruption, it needs to be actualized in physical terms. And if it is an actual physical disruption, then, it is purely physical.

The point of our discussion is that the gateway locale is fundamentally required by infrastructure so that it is the true reception of infrastructure; it is nuanced and genuine. This is why comedy is a very genuine outlook on current infrastructure: it must work with the assumed reality, and any deviation from the assumed reality would cause one not to enter completely and therefore not lose themselves within it to enter the punchline of a new reality.

Doorway and Disrupted Continuity

The doorway is a place between places, which connects one side to another. It does so from its point of view which does not want to be named in any other way other than its opposing sides. This humility, removing its namesake in order to allow for each side to connect to the other, is why it becomes overlooked as a habitat of regard. When it accentuates itself then it becomes a divide from both sides and takes the form of a third space. When it is insufficiently situated then it will provide limited access to either side and become an obstruction of interaction and space.

To define the doorway we must first perceive two rooms that are side-by-side for further examination. When we understand that housing is an embodied experience of an enclosement that conceptually retains human consciousness from externalities, then we understand that entering into the doorway would create a strong reduction of that experience or in other words would be a loss of embodiment. In dramatic terms, in the sequence of consciousness, the exit or entrance is a situational death. Consciousness cannot move between contextual domains because it must utilize certain ground to remain in continuity with each other.

The contextual grounding is the life-force of consciousness in which the change of domains is a contextual transition. The particulars on the dearth of consciousness pertain to the receptivity between those domains. This would be another room in a house or the gate of a city or country. The dearth of consciousness experienced in the departure from the gate of the city, especially if the other side does not retain elements of the city, would be drastic and existential. While the movement from room to room in a house will have an existential effect, it is not considered a loss of consciousness but more like a conscious skip.

If we are to be exact, even in the same room, in the same space, consciousness can experience dearth by disrupting its flow with illogicality or illogical physical activity. Unless there is no change to the physical domain in which one is situated, consciousness should continue indefinitely. However, if an individual follows their attention towards aspects or elements which do not pertain to a sequential pattern then consciousness cannot continue.

This is why long periods in a stagnant location will cause one to 'space-out' or obsessively attend or un-attend to an element or aspect. They are not interested in the point of attention but are very interested in not being interested; in this fashion to be able to resist the sequential movement of the psyche with a focal point which serves to dismiss. We cannot dismiss consciousness without a tangible ground, and the focal point in the physical realm will provide a ground to become ungrounded. It is as if the ground is removed for a moment; that the returned pattern is not in connection with the previous one. This is a conceptual doorway.

Because the doorway must be anonymous to the interaction it becomes a place of habitual forgetfulness. It cannot adorn us with automatic movement from one side to the other in complete unity. The intent of unifying and being continuous will create a specific domain for the doorway, particularly looking relevant but remote for its purpose of transition. What will become is that one room will be projected onto the other or the second room will overtake the first.

The projection occurs because when assumed that the transition is yet a continuous motion, the conceptualization that is gained in the current room will become an attempted experience throughout the entire system of movement. What is lost because of the transition is due to an unavailability to any specific ground. For where is the conscious material grounded? If in the inner room then it will be unavailable outside of it, if in the doorway, then not an emanation from the inner room, and if in the outer room then it has no relation to the doorway or inner room.

Such projection might seem like a fertile attempt at obtaining a conscious flow that is not disrupted and can enjoy inconsistencies across a spectrum. We could even imagine certain success from following the conscious flow. Within the doorway one partakes in deliberations that have arrived from the inner room. The problem arises in the entrance to the next room which is a certain contextual formula that does not agree with preceding events. This will be a natural conflict to whatever one is proposing to thrust onto the system. For a time it would seem successful, where a healthy conflict of prior consciousness and current consciousness are in disagreement yet in agreement to such.

However, as time is extended it results that one has physically entered into that domain but is conceptually not in agreement to the entering phase at all. For the psyche, the conflict is not so much the conscious flow but the reality of the situation. One is persistent in continuing as if not to be where they are; and every form of physicality which surrounds them are distractions from their memory that nostalgically attaches to non-physical memories.

The ability to navigate this next room is only due to its representation of prior physicality, which the psyche brings to forebear in its ability to interact with current dealings. Every interaction will be sub-layered to a representative in memory of previous physicality and would be highly costly to energy consumption. Even the agreement of interacting at all with current physicality is inconsistent, for one has not conceptually entered, there should be no reason to interact with a particulars of that entrance.

This allowance for the inconsistency reveals an importance of intro-perceptive and extro-perceptive interactions. In fact, a conceptual trick is in play, where memory and its nostalgic attachments are unable to simply arise. They must attach to representatives of present interactions for its revealed experience. Theoretically, one can attach to a memory without clear physical interactions but there is something—somewhere that is assisting to bring this about. When one is enclosed in a tight sealed chamber without physical objects, they will find it difficult to proceed to their memory in concession.

The hypocritical nature is quite apparent, being that the current physical domain is both being ignored for its details but being used to allow a memory to remain vitalized. Furthermore, that memory which current physicality offers vitality is being used to disallow the current physicality from appearing in true existence. We could realize such a cycle as disruptive to the psyche, energy consumption, and sociality.

Every relationship dynamic during this interplay of inconsistencies will be to either represent the nostalgic time period or to demand an exposition on the reality that stands in front of them. There is the promising depth of those relationships, for without connection to a reality, the details that follow cannot be attempted or revealed. Even as the dynamics seem illustrious and existentially demanding, they are only in service to the existential disparity of their inconsistent alignment to reality. We may wonder as to the benefit of such relationships from the opposing standpoint, and this would be revealed from the very struggle that is exposed to others as well.

Even as one resides in their domain for an extended period, they find its connection to the doorways which lead outwards to have been tampered. And following the dynamic of a person in such a discrepancy, they allow themselves to attempt it, participating in a larger domain that has seemingly been shut off. Those that provide cushion to continue in the nostalgic framework are doing so because it cannot be imagined to relinquish the domain which they arrive from. They are also being revealed to the notion that exile from a current domain always provides insight into details that are lost to one who has remained centric to their domain. It is that very notion that threatens the stability of their continuity and future. And as they attempt to have their relationships continue to project their nostalgic attachment to current reality, they hope to prove that exile is not a relevancy for their centric position. This provides an interesting insight into dynamic relationships, which are representatives of domains in succession from one another. Had the populace been exposed to the continuity of all domains there would not be a need for such relationships. Thus, people represent domains in their interactions with other domains.

Masculinity and the Doorway

There is something to be said for the prospect of entering the doorway in its disruption of a prior environmental setting. There is a shedding of all systems when the choice is made to follow the doorway, in reference to consciousness arriving at a complete loss. Therefore, the process of utilizing the doorway is already leaning toward a masculine outlook, to which it halts feminine expression and its vitality so that a new formation can be made. We could not say with earnestness that there is a feminine expression in the usage of any doorway, and it will always expose the realization that one is not all they appear to be, as if the entire feminine database is somehow a weighty burden for the process, and all present cannot appreciate the expense nor the sentimental value.

The doorway is a harsh movement that is consistent with war and other sorts, which will always be masculine by its chosen demarcation despite possibility and development. Losing an environment is not only a change of pace but a systematic differentiation. The prior space is a habitat which serves the psyche for its compartment of distinct measures. Those measures serve domestication toward the presence of certain material and no other. The partnership allow the psyche to retain a presentation of those measures for the purpose of participation without renunciation. The departure from the doorway is an immediate loss of domestication, resulting from renouncing that participation, without the hopeful possibility that it will be carried along.

Domestication cannot follow through the doorway because it does not retain any value other than a reminder of what lies behind a sentiment or what is to follow. The moment of exit is truly an exit, and even as the doorway retains a capsule of the prior state, it is doing so from a place of memory and not perceptual data. This is why the material of domestication within a doorway will be fading and choppy, because it has the claim of nearness to the perceptual data while also being defined as something that differentiates it from that realm.

Therefore, the doorway is a masculine trait by renouncing any prior engagements without the possibility of further developments to justify it. It is thus masculinity that only disrupts femininity and does not further the aim toward a charged formation which would stimulate what was lost previously. Until the next destination, there is an existential loss in its entirety.

Because of this one-sided disposition, without the possibility of feminine expression, the doorway is regarded with a certain humility toward such imbalance. A denunciation is therefore needed to be enjoined without so much as notice of its process. The entire doorway system is one which should remain behind the realm of consciousness because it exposes an imbalance of nature. The same is applicable of warfare, which does great forms of denunciation of any prior life relevance but does not know what will come from the expense. This is the reason that the proper approach to the doorway is not to make one aware of all that is said or will be said in the present work. It must follow at the loss of any conscious engagement, because first, consciousness will drag what was already lost, and secondly, consciousness will uncover a presence of masculinity without regard for femininity.

In other words, there is no dynamical exchange between individuals, and as such one cannot even engage in internal dialogue, which is an abridged version of sociality. For what conversation could be had when it is not available to feminine regard? Just as in warfare, there is no purpose to dynamical exchange because its very presence is the neglect of any reference to feminine reciprocation. In certain terms, it is not even considered masculinity, but rather the rawness of biological matter which does not contain a conscious decoder. Masculinity is only granted to those that entertain a feminine reception of certain regard, and in this case there is no such element; it is only considered deficient sociality, whether external or internal. The engagements that may be entertained, for whatever reason, will always contain a troubling imbalance between speaker and receiver, to which no one will want to take the role of doorway within the conversation.

The doorway is a representation of the human dynamic and would be to disregard conceptual forms. When one attempts an engagement, the proper reciprocation would be to disregard the entire engagement, as would the doorway. Instead, one will engage irrespective of the proper dynamic and take the role of another conceptual role that does not pertain to the present needs of both parties. The needs of every human within a doorway is the representation of the doorway, which, if spoken for, will say that the entire conscious enterprise is null and void and spoken language is quite irrelevant, unless for immediate movement toward a real-time destination.

Domains, Foundations, and Conceptual Disagreement

Even within a current domain, there is agreement to its reality and its connection to other domains; their relationship will represent conceptual demands of a certain kind. When one individual enters into a realm of conceptual depth, they will be a representation to the other of its availability. The other may disagree by noting the problematic disruptions of the present domain or how the succeeding domain is not an overall conceptual enlargement. The problem with making a claim on a promising domain is that the coinciding individual has already entered and would be staking against reality. If they are successful in disrupting their connection to that domain, it does dissolve that domain from consciousness. The only claim is that the new domain is not a conceptual gain, by displaying the details that prove such. The only one who could do such is one who has entered as well, being that they are existentially familiar with it.

The outside vantage point will not provide those details, and the matter that can arise is the apparent vulnerabilities that appear from the outside. They will make a conceptual point in those details but will not be following a conceptual argument in its entirety. For every conceptual domain has vulnerabilities which are fairly apparent to the simplistic bystander. This is a dynamic relationship which, on one side, exposes the weakness that does not *know* the reality, and the other hopes that in having one follow that argument, they have obtained that domain without existentially partaking in it. For if they placed an argument that had one reconcile, then it proves that they contain that domain in its entirety and still persist in the present domain.

This is not the reality of affairs, and instead they contain no new substance than a bystander who identifies vulnerabilities. The claim of their domain is usually short-lived because, although the other individual followed their argument, they will still contain the existential nature of that domain in its entirety. Eventually, they will not bow to the vulnerability and will naturally reenter the domain as if having not left. This will then prove to the other side of the dynamic that they do not contain the domain, for their proof was that the vulnerability was a thorough argument when it was a fraction of the entire domain.

Dependency and Passage

There is much to know about the doorway, but its most important attribute is where its origin and destination. The path to which the doorway is found must be of a certain parameter, which when unsuccessful will not prove to be the doorway nor the emanation of propagation from its domain. For instance, a room that does not have any connecting space to other parts of a home structure will not emanate its presence into the rest of the structure. Of course, being a part of an existing structure will grant a certain emanation, but this is drastically diminished when there is no pocket of physical interaction.

If we were to construct a very large building, the interaction between rooms without open pathways will only be in exchange to a very limited eminence, much like sharing similarities of structure and space more than stable exchange. The most elementary point of exchange is the foundation, which is conceived at the root and adheres to the same stable ground despite variation in space. When we change this single point and perform separate foundations, for instance on two sides of a road, the connection through structural engineering will not replicate.

Foundations are the highest consideration because all space is in reference to ground. It is not about the shared connection of materials or structural design but in reference to what they all rest upon and are dependent on: the ground. A foundation cannot be considered in its parts because it relies on its structural dependencies and all the portions of ground on which it depends. Dependency is the trait because gravity is the law of nature which forces space on location. When this is not the case as in an airplane, as the dependency moves from ground to the mechanized system, which becomes its *ground* until it grounds. The plane is allowed its spatial locale because of its mechanization, which if lost will remove the space it inhabits, and the initial ground will be its next host.

Locale is granted by dependency in whatever element of nature we deal with. That dependency will be the character of the entire structure, so that a plane will be a showcase of mechanization and the majority of its points of consciousness will be based on that. As well, we must consider the drivers of such mechanization, who are recognized as individuals upon whom the rest are dependent. Being in such a prominent position requires that they mirror that sentiment with an expectation that is not demanded of any other trade or skill, even that of the medical field. Only because they serve as the dependency of space that is being inhabited are they expected to that level of dedication.

If we identify portions in which the foundation is not dependent, then it will not be considered. For instance, the structure is built depending on the foundation, which is dependent on the ground. When we add an additional space to its intrinsic foundation, then it will not gain independence with the rest of the structure. It is not so much the dependency of the foundation but its connection as its dependable or vulnerable portion. The primary characteristic of a foundation is its dependency on ground, for the ground is the primary point in any structure. However, the dependability itself is not primary, but rather that we structure around that dependability so that all of the foundation will be included as long as it is connected through structural design.

We will not assume the first floor is part of the foundation even as it is connected structurally to the foundation. The dependency is liberal to the structural design, since we do not see any connection of dependency for it only rests upon the foundation. If the foundation is structurally sufficient in only a portion and continues to a non-dependable foundation, it will be classed into the same dependency because, upon the decline of its own failing, will utilize those connections for minuscule dependencies. When we layer upon a structure, it will not provide any sort of structural cushion in its connection to the ground. When there is a part of a foundation that is completely dismembered from dependency on the ground, then whatever goes on top of it will be dependent on the original foundation for its stability. Thus, we have a ground and its dependencies of a structure, which is the core independence of a building and its distribution of eminencies.

When not structurally dependent or attached, we begin to provide names for each side. Structures that are immensely bigger will not maintain such naming divisions. The name is to provide a certain ample provision to what seems to be lost from the loss of its shared foundation. The name grants both the recognition of independence and the structural connection of a certain floor, which gives it a right to be under the same general description. Even as this may be a narrow hallway, its provision of social movement without leaving the confines of the structure gives it a conceptual recognition that constitutes it as a single entity. This is only the right of sociality to recognize their spatial availability, but in terms of the structured eminence of interaction, the portions will have a different disposition, as can be testified through social experience.

This is immediately downgraded when the structural connection is underground, which provides the same access to social movement. Because the connection is below the foundational element and its dependency, it grants both more homogeneity to the connection itself but less to the coinciding buildings. Such that we will be at odds over naming underground connections as being of the same structure, as certain cities may have the right to be named a single structure.

The underground dimension gives it its peculiar identification as a vestibule, which has homogeneity in itself. The underground connection becomes a doorway between buildings but not a direct connection; the doorway becomes upgraded to the status of vestibule in which it takes its own meaning seriously. This is where its homogeneous nature, of being a proper doorway, limits the exposure of either side but adheres to the transfer of eminence. This becomes a powerful variation which grants continued structural eminence between all of its access points but does not overbear as a direct connection. This makes independence a trifling ordeal, for we cannot bear the details of continuous connection. The exhaustion will play out and the eminence will become lost in the space itself, which can occur for a variety of reasons.

The access points of the underground connections are bound to its doorways that link up to the external realm. Those access points act like any other doorway in defining the eminence of the vestibule's containment and emanation outward to the other access points. The most contained vestibule is also the one that will disallow a rumination of eminence, while the most uncontained vestibule will provide direct connection which will not exchange, but will be as if the doorway does not exist and the two rooms are directly in connection.

Within a space itself, eminence can be lost through exhaustion, either by making the structural assumption of great eminence but not being delivered such, or the self-denigrating humility of being unaware of the eminence that flows through it.

In the case of structural assumption, the eminence will not be available for experience or continuation, while the self-denigrating structure will retain such but will not be extracted by normal use or experience. Similar to the human who displays extravagance that is not in participation with their internal depth, which if extended to its furthest point will cause the extravagance to have them lost to the existential depth that was already obtained.

Conscious Flow and Biological Experience

We could perceive the inner room as a ruminating consciousness that enters a domain in service of such. What consciousness lacks of most pressing urgency is the biological layer, being that it is a construct of the mind which hovers the biological entity. To provide for this, at intervals there must be a removal of consciousness to interact with biological experience. Because nothing can be interacted without a conscious overlay, we are propelled into a paradox of impossible resolution. The resolution can begin coming to a head when we interact with the biological layer in its most interactive element, disintegrated from conscious flow. This would mean that the only reason we are interacting with this interactive element is because of its natural biological curiosity. There is no conscious motivation or intention that leads us to interact, but only biological, as would be a biological determination.

The problem begins when we attempt to interact with the biological aspect for the sake of such, when we meet our own destitution in the inability to substantiate any relevant information other than biological experience. Therefore, we arrive at a sort of compromise in which we first and foremost disrupt conscious flow, and then naturally arrive at biological layers that are worthwhile of interaction. When we interact with whatever substance, we are doing so because it is manifest material and not consciously ordained. Still, another compromise is needed because interactive substance arises without sensitivity to coordination and contextual binding. Indeed, we must apply a contextual layer upon the biological interactive substance in order to supersede it with substantial material that could gain our interest. Without these contextual layers upon the biological interactions, we would fall deeply into interaction to perform a biological experience or reflection without any sort of material that can interact with overall consciousness when that is brought to vitality.

Careful deliberation is in order that the interactive substance arises as manifest material and not consciously ordained, which then can be proposed with contextual layers. These layers are noticeably going to manifest from background consciousness, but will do so in the interest of the interactive substance. Therefore, deliberation is in order at each moment to identify if it is the interactive substance which is the basis of the experience and the contextual aspect as a provision, or if the interactive experience is being utilized to produce more conscious flow that would uphold or ignore the reality of the biological layer; as would a biological experience immediately be a sign of certain conscious deliberations. The biological moment or experience is immediately passed to prove a point on the conscious continuum and is not interacted for its own sake, in which the contextual layers are only to provide cushion or through-lines to interact with that reality and its true form.

It can always be identified when one interacts with the familial body from either the vantage point to prove continuing consciousness, or interactions which require contextual layers from consciousness to experience the biological self away from, and sometimes in opposition to, consciousness. Naturally, what is obtained in the conscious realm will seep into any interactive experience of the biological self and will do so in its own time. Because all experience is directly derivative of conscious flow, it is only a matter of time before biological interactions will have that appearance. But in this discussion, we are concluding that from the vantage point of consciousness we cannot access the biological experience, but in the trust that biological experience, even in opposition to consciousness, will receive conscious flow provided that it is substantial and existential through the interactive structure.

The doorway is the reception of a degradation of consciousness which can be designated as a highly volatile interactive structure. It cannot be interacted in its intrinsic domain because it is utilized only as a method of disruption from a singular conscious flow to another. It is a safe assurance that it is an interactive domain that spans both sides of the door despite its intrinsic nature. There is a necessary trust in the structure that it will not be inhabited with distinctiveness but will be an abridged version of both sides of its domain. For the sake of reference, we cannot imagine a doorway that leads to three distinct locations, as the more dominant two will be the manifestation of its domain. The third entrance will be neglected as a contribution to the doorway and will only provide definition to the other two entrances.

The only time that it is worthwhile to interact with the doorway is after the matter, because of its vital nature. The door is both serving as an interactive structure and as a transition from the expiry of consciousness onwards to further consciousness or to interactive structures, and when interacted with at the time being will not allow the bridging contrast to occur. Instead, the interactive structure proves itself worthwhile and will be obtainable in interacting with consciousness; from either side of the door and will not be providing its ultimate service of transitioning consciousness. When the doorway is overly interacted with, then conscious expiry is complete and absolute, and whatever is attempting from the other side toward former consciousness would be in service of a memory, not of a continuing existential reality.

Thus, the doorway provides a disadvantage so that the conscious reality from one side continues to be a reality on the other. For even though the interactive details of its own domain are lost and not experienced as a conscious entity in any reality, it is worthwhile under the assumption that connecting the conscious flow on either side is the better service of the two. The doorway must be served through memory, which will not make it a conscious reality but will serve as an interactive experience that can promote details of either side of the door. When the memory is not followed, then the interactive structure within the doorway will become a dominant portion of reality by its neglectful and vulnerable state. It is a reality, but has been barred from deliberation when on goings are present. Such vulnerabilities attached to the existential nature will seek retribution at a later date, that is, if not interacted with by virtue of memory, which will grant those details relevancy, importance, and overall conscious structure.

Gateway of Sociality: Performance and Politics

There is a requisite of a gateway or entranceway to participate in its inhabited structure. But in this way, it must fundamentally orient itself in the compartmentalization that it finds itself within that compound. For if it proceeds to develop a streamlined connection to a specific compartment or attribute of the internal structure, it will be disoriented.

The reason that this is not sought in its first instance, in every structure, is that there is a detriment to the inhabitants partaking in the orientation of its gateway, and it supposes itself to correlate with the sentiment of the inhabitant, all the while proposing a performance to the activity that undergoes the gateway. One is supposing themselves as a representation of themselves and will automatically be unparalleled to the actuality of that process, or to the need of performance that has specific attributes that do not correlate with the specificity of the inhabitants.

Thus, the only manner in which this imitative form of sociality is well performed is through the activity that is characteristic of a performance; specifically, that of the performative function as though it is arbitrary to the content and rather to embody what is not able or normal to be embodied, and distant from what concerns direct sociality. A performance is thus the specifically role-bearing mold that is requisite for a political orientation, where it represents itself as the sociality contained within the inhabiting structure.

The performance is to orient the roles of what is within the inhabiting structure to gain semblance of its conciliatory information. If the case is overtly narrow, without the articulation of what supposes the internal manifestation, or if it is too broad, in which it is removed from that duality and allows for a continuity between what is external and what is eternal, then it will not be constituted as a gateway unless it loses its characteristics.

In the case of no orientation between the compartmentalization from within the structure and what is outside it, the gateway constitutes a continuing sociality from within its realm and propagates outwardly, but this occurs at the expense of the broader duality between what is external to it and the way it manifests itself in its internal mainframe. It acts as though the sociality that continues from outside is a single sequence to the compartmentalization from within. And because this is not the genuine nature of that process, either the internal realm overwhelms itself with external information by virtue of not realizing its differentiation, or becomes habituated without a concurrent sequence for that sociality that continues onward from outside its mainframe; it is viewed disproportionately to enable information to continue.

Yet we have ample evidence for this proposition, since most households do not have a specific orientation of their gateway, unless we suppose that the household is following a duality concurrent throughout its structure; that of representing itself while performing, while continuing, as it were, in its compartmentalization. And if that were the case, then the duality within the household becomes detrimental from within itself, where it is continuously representing the very information that it seeks to propositionalize, or, in the other case, propositionalizing against the manner in which it needs to be represented. But in the regular case, where such is not the case, the household will either go to the extreme end of either spectrum: either to overwhelm itself or to underwhelm itself, since the gateway is lacking its supposed material for performing as a political characteristic between external sociality and internal compartmentalization.

The very problem of orienting the purposeful endeavor of creating a gateway is that it enables the political orientation of such, which also has, as its disposition, the ability to go to the extreme in its political activation; either to be deterred from all sociality and thus perform as the perfect political function but be detrimental to the purpose of the gateway, or to the other extreme of allowing an inhabiting state from outside the sociality to within, ignoring the stature required to separate such and enable the gateway as a formative function.

As we mentioned, the natural supposition of a gateway is the deterrence of sociality, so that it is actually the endeavor to propose itself not as a deterrence, but as an acquisition and proposition between two points of sociality that do not have a sufficient connection to each other. It requires the performance of sociality to do this, for if it inhabits the desert-like state of no sociality, then it will not gain entrance from outside sociality, nor articulate the internal compartmentalization for the attachment of what is external to it. However, this performance can only be provided if it acts out the roles of both the constituents from within its realm, as well as its receptive behavior to what is external to it. Since such a performance is, by definition, allocated to the receiving end rather than another way of performing for the acquisition of sociality, there is no acquisition of sociality; it is dependent on the compartmentalization from within the structure, and dependent on the external sociality to orient that information, rather than external sociality being dependent on what is internal to it.

This is the very nature and design of a gateway: it attempts to suppose to the external realm some level of performance in how it partakes from within its domain. It attempts to activate a sort of representation, but more so than a representation, a performance, so that the natural deterrence of a gateway does not prevent sociality from contracting with the internal mainframe. In the case of strong political institutions, this is at a certain detriment, since the gateway is a deterrence, as well as the performance being such that it deters by the sentimental value of political prowess, all the more so with the sociality that inhabits the gateway to provide deterrence, to a point where there is no continuity between the sociality external to it and what is internal. Every level of performance is only to its detriment, rather than to the acquisition of that sociality. In the case of a political institution that works to perform as an institutional function separate from sociality, this is its intended process. However, in the case where the political institution is to perform as a political agent, this is detrimental, for how can a political agent be disproportionate from the sociality which they represent, and for which the duality of their embodiment is non-existent?

In contrast to the political orientation in general, which is also a modality of duality, where there is no sociality from within its mainframe, but only the continuity of regular social systems, as well as the perspective of social need, the duality of both what the social requisite is thus far, plus attention to the current and procedural sociality, creates a duality of those two realms. In the case of detachment from direct sociality, or detachment from the compositional theme of acting as a representational element of the overall requisite of the political body, it will either be an authoritarian, or, in the former case, a baseless political orientation that is political in name only, but most like a regular conceptual process of sociality, such as an eatery.

It might be attempted to say that the political orientation is a gateway, and the gateway is fundamentally political. However, that is an overstatement, for the outcome or purpose of a gateway is to provide continuity to two social forms that otherwise would not be continuous, for there is a dearth of separation by its structure, by its differing sociality, that it would not be able to mend. In the case of a political orientation, it is the oversight of systemic bodies that can move within and without sociality without the detriment of the mobility of concurrent sociality that would cause it to deflect itself from oversight, more so to remain in oversight. This occurs all the while staying connected to a representational element of what is concurrent in sociality. Its intended outcome is not to bridge between two social forms, but rather to allow oversight that is not conflated with sociality. However, in the case of duality, they remain the same: to suppose an unavailable sociality from within its domain; but in the case of the gateway, to perform sociality; in the case of the political orientation, to compound sociality, to move from within and without its structure.

The gateway is perfected only when the sociality external to it, or the compartmentalization within its structure, is unavailable for attendance, so that it becomes increasingly reliant upon the convergence between those two realms. In the case of its most detrimental lack of stimulation or social performance in each of those realms, the gateway serves not only as the allowance of continuing sociality, but rather in the way that sociality functions in itself, in its proper orientation.

Since the gateway is a performance, the duality of the dearth of sociality between its two sides, when sociality is lacking transparency or functionality on either side, results not in a performance, but in habituation, becoming the locality from which it succeeds as a construct of liminal sociality within its own state. It is not because it stops acting as a gateway, but because the inputted sociality on either side does not allow for convergence, since there is no duality other than the ability to aggregate information from within its own platform. Aggregation is not the same as convergence of a duality, for it grosses information that does not correlate and does not succeed as a dialogical stature between sociality, but inhabits the details, or betterments of those details, to gain a functioning platform of information that succeeds to represent, in a streamlined manner, not between itself, but in how it performs between that sociality.

The last venture of a detriment of sociality is its gateway, because as sociality that is internal or external to it degenerates, what remains is how it attempts to correlate from one part to another. Thus, the gateway is its last vestige. In the gateway, it takes hold of any and all social aspects that do not perform in their own right, for they are degenerate in its locality. But because it is removed from the locality from which they degenerate, its best vestiges lie dormant for the gateway to acquiesce, as well, in the external form of that gateway, which performs just the same and whose vestiges lie dormant at the gateway, inhabiting only that which is the gateway.

If we view civilizations at their most degenerate form, it is the gateway that stands last, because when all sociality has degenerated, it attempts its last performance to converge with other sociality, to aggregate itself to something beyond itself, or to itself that has been in detriment for a long time and now attempts to offer its last remnants beyond itself. It does not go so far as to reach beyond, because it is degenerate, remaining in that liminal space of the gateway, attempting to extrapolate its last aspects of sociality. The same is true for external sociality, which is another realm that does not stand on its own and now enables itself to perform the function of convergence, at least to something other than itself, which is not received on the other end, because convergence is imperfect, but whose vestiges lie dormant and available for the gateway to that eternal function.

What in its regular day is simply a performance of the roles of sociality and its compartmentalization within a structure has now become non-performative; rather, the only venture of sociality for itself. This is evident in the general notion of a performance, which in its regular case is an attempted aggregation of sociality in its deviating manner. But when sociality declines to a vital level, what is left is not the performance, but the only access point to sociality from which to gain any ascendancy. Likewise, a society focused on performance as its only measure, or an individual focused on the performative function of their individuality, is at its last vestige of sociality, from which the only access point is how it embodies a role outside of that sociality; almost as if to contain whatever is finally going to be lost in a deviating role, articulate only because it is not sociality itself and is declining in the performance itself.

Perspective, Diversity, and Imagination

Imagination still requires something which a container cannot provide, that of perspective. Perspective is another way of saying "the ability to see from various angles." This becomes possible by the two elements: that of a letdown of infrastructure and diverse elements for the usage of differentiated sight. When we have infrastructure that is to the tee, then even with diverse elements, they will not stand out on their own; meaning the lens of the glasses will be bound by the entire system.

For instance, in a train car as opposed to a house overlooking a train car, the diverse elements are still amicable within the train, but because it is system-bound, it cannot be used on its own. Even if one was able to isolate away from the system, it still ruminates in the background so that one cannot walk away relaying that they had the ability of perspective within the train but only that they saw it a certain way. The difference is that the other way is not like the individual who is scanning screens to choose a perspective from a neutral point of view. This is why infrastructure can never fully provide the experience of a gateway, for instance, an airport, rest station, etc.

The second element is diversity, so that even when detached from infrastructure, there must be elements that provide the screening of that perspective but that are specialized to reach back to infrastructure. The most pertinent example of this is the beach or bodies of water in general. They have the required element of diversity, the horizon, which holds the ability of many directions, and is connected back to infrastructure so that the 'horizon' or the diversity of view is connected to the locale or container that can lead to that in many ways. A horizon that is isolated from infrastructure does not bear that strong of an effect, for it is a perspective for something that is not bearing an elemental station.

In fact, all imagination, irrespective of geographical structure, is required with these two elements, amongst other things. It must have the ability of diversity, so that one that is under duress will not have a very liminal imagination, for the diversity of perspective is not existent as the container or the system that is in place is too stimulating; too structured. As well, with the disconnection but limited attachment to those parts of the psyche.

This would mean that imagination is most telling when one does not bind themselves to their state of mind but also remains anchored and tethered to a pathway that leads to a concrete state of mind. When imagination runs wild, it has become untethered and also is less creative and more erratic. On the contrary, when imagination is too stationary, like the corporeal structure for creativity, it becomes almost identical to the thing itself and thus can be considered a weak creation.

Creation in general is the same affair; it must be tethered to the previous state of being, but also separated so that it can be available in its own sphere. As well, creation must contain an availability of diversity of perspective, which will provide pathways outward to the horizon. We can often find creation that has the first element but lacks the second, where because of some inability and preoccupation, there is no diversity to the imagination, so that it is separated but not in depth. Also, even as one is an internal being, one still needs external references to be the provision of that channel to those perspectives; one needs a physical horizon to emulate that diversity.

For example, a tradition of the form of creative arts, which offers scope to these perspectives. In real creation, one needs to create channels within themselves to provide for the horizon, meaning erratic embodiments of different formations, not for the necessity of creating any of them but to give sense to the physical channels which allow the diversity of imagination to settle upon. In our case, this would be the gateway locale, which in regular terms is antithetical to all regular systems, antithetical to both infrastructure (which it is not) and the imagination (which is not real). But, this very trait makes it so necessary for the development of both infrastructure and man.

Infrastructure needs makeshift infrastructures that are separated as required by the elements maintained, so that the imagination can become regulated. We will find in any sophisticated infrastructural setting the antiquated systems that served as this required, which then became a part of the infrastructure so that it cannot be noticed forthright. Examples include rivers, tunnels, dams, and other formations that could have served as gateways, which still do, but only in an infrastructural sense and not in the true ability of a gateway.

We find a major innovation from the body of water and beach, which provide a buffer that can never be incorporated into infrastructure, so that it remains a gateway locale even as infrastructure is toppled upon it. For this reason, we find them together, that of water and infrastructure; besides the biological reasons, there is the provision of a gateway that allows for an imagination despite the infrastructural setting

www.ingramcontent.com/pod-product-compliance
Lightning Source LLC
Chambersburg PA
CBHW062133040426
42335CB00039B/2083